Cássio Remus de Paula

Video games and World War II: The conflict in virtual representations

Cássio Remus de Paula

Video games and World War II: The conflict in virtual representations

An iconographic and iconological study of electronic games dealing with the war between the Axis and the Allies

ScienciaScripts

Imprint
Any brand names and product names mentioned in this book are subject to trademark, brand or patent protection and are trademarks or registered trademarks of their respective holders. The use of brand names, product names, common names, trade names, product descriptions etc. even without a particular marking in this work is in no way to be construed to mean that such names may be regarded as unrestricted in respect of trademark and brand protection legislation and could thus be used by anyone.

Cover image: www.ingimage.com

This book is a translation from the original published under ISBN 978-3-330-76400-2.

Publisher:
Sciencia Scripts
is a trademark of
Dodo Books Indian Ocean Ltd. and OmniScriptum S.R.L publishing group

120 High Road, East Finchley, London, N2 9ED, United Kingdom
Str. Armeneasca 28/1, office 1, Chisinau MD-2012, Republic of Moldova, Europe
Managing Directors: Ieva Konstantinova, Victoria Ursu
info@omniscriptum.com

Printed at: see last page
ISBN: 978-620-8-40786-5

Index

CHAPTER 1 2

CHAPTER 2 16

CHAPTER 3 35

CHAPTER 4 72

CHAPTER 1

The "video game" object

On the praxis of play: cultural or natural inheritance?

Although slowly and gradually, it was the advent of the Annales[1] in 1929 that made it possible to use research objects that went far beyond scholarly texts that sought to find the "truth" of history. One of the legacies of this movement was the expansion of cultural history during the 1980s and 1990s. In this way, many historians sought to define more specific sections for their research objects, resulting in works such as "the culture of merit", "the culture of the company", "the culture of secrecy" and even "the culture of gambling"; in other words, from then on it became possible to write about a "cultural history of everything". The methods of historical research that had previously catered only for art or science also came to cater for studies of practices - such as talking, reading or playing (BURKE, 2008, p.43-46). In this way, cultural history came to suggest "to other cultural scholars new ideas about the innumerable ways in which the various aspects of a civilisation can interact" (GOMBRICH, 1994, p.91).

The practice of playing, in turn, has generated a discussion about its origins, which has resulted in two perspectives: one natural and the other cultural. The historian Johann Huizinga discusses these aspects best. With regard to the theory that refers to nature, the historian exemplifies the practice of play with dogs that follow rules and a pattern of gestures while playing: they don't bite each other's ears, at least not violently. "They pretend to be angry and, what is most important, they evidently experience immense pleasure and amusement in all this" (HUIZINGA, 2000, p.5). By following this ritual, they know that any cheating during the play activity means the end of the

[1] An academic movement that emerged in France, founded by Lucien Febvre and Marc Bloch, first as a journal and over the next decade as a school. Annales aimed to break away from history as a positivist element, approaching the Social Sciences to propose, for example, questions about culture, mentalities and representations (BURKE, 2008, p.11).

game. In other words, the practice of play can be attributed to a heritage essentially linked to the activities of nature: aren't two plants playing for survival by trying to reach the sunlight directly? After all, competitiveness is the essence of survival, which extends from the least complex creatures in the Fungi kingdom to man.

In opposition to this theory, it is suggested that games are a cultural construction. From childhood, we learn to play with words, for example; or, instead of attributing playful practice to learning, we can associate it with simulation: lovers, for example, who unconsciously create virtual emotions; feelings that aren't, just to successfully fulfil the need to pretend (DUVIGNAUD, 1997, p.33).

From this perspective, it is understood that the praxis of play is linked to ludic activities constructed by humanity. Still in line with Huizinga, this time suggesting that play can be an attribute of culture, Sérgio Gallo explains that

> (...) all the great instinctive forces of civilised life have their origin in myth and in the "primeval soil of play": law and order, commerce and profit, industry, art, poetry, philosophy, knowledge and science. The great archetypal activities of human society have, since their inception, been entirely marked by play, as has language itself, because every abstract expression carries a hidden metaphor, and every metaphor is a play on words (GALLO, 2007, p.22-23).

The idea is that play is inherent in the construction of civilisations and social practices; in short, a civilisation can be defined by its preferred play practices and vice versa. For example, it's not surprising that in many of the city-states of ancient Greece, bodybuilding was admired; the cult of the body and combat led that civilisation to praise competitiveness through the Olympic Games. Wrestling, throwing and running were disciplines honoured every four years (BLAINEY, 2008, p.68). The game is, in short, a reflection of the identity of a particular civilisation. Caillois emphasises this idea, arguing that:

> There is, in fact, a growing affinity between the rules of games and the qualities and defects of the members of a community. These games (...) manifest, on the one hand, the most common tendencies, tastes and ways of thinking and, at the same time, educate and train the players in these same virtues and errors, sanctioning in them habits and preferences. In such a way that a game that a certain people favour can, in turn, serve to define some of

their moral and intellectual traits (CAILLOIS, 1990, p.102).

Based on the assumption that the practice of play is a culturally constructed attribute, it's no mistake to say that, in turn, it simulates aspects that derive from nature. Therefore, it seems erroneous from a logical point of view that there is a "right" and a "wrong" aspect; its *praxis is* a hybrid of nature and culture.

The iconological-iconographic method

"Iconology" and "iconography" are concepts of analysis applied to static images that seek, in general terms, to interpret the representations and symbologies contained in certain figures. The concern to obtain results of historical interpretation through images arose during the 1920s and 1930s with the so-called art historians. They argued that works of art should be seen as texts, since they were not painted simply to be observed - but read. Among these art historians - along with the philosopher Ernst Cassirer - were the Hamburg Germans Aby Warburg, Fritz Saxl, Erwin Panofsky and Edgar Wind, the group responsible for creating the Warburg School (BURKE, 2004, p.43-45).

In an essay published in 1939, Panofsky explained how the iconological and iconographic process of an image was carried out. In order for the image to be successfully analysed, the historian had to pay attention to three levels of interpretation: the pre-iconographic description, which looks at the items and objects present in the painting (or photograph); the events, an item that implies the context presented in the image (battles, ceremonies, etc.); and finally, the most important, which is the "intrinsic meaning", in other words, the symbols that reveal the identity of a nation, among its religious and military precepts, customs, practices, clothing, etc. The triple interpretative proposed by Panofsky made up the notion of visual hermeneutics[2] , or iconology (BURKE, 2004, p.45; PANOFSKY, 1986, p.47-65). More precisely, "before trying to read images 'between the lines', and to use them as historical evidence, it is

[2] "Hermeneutics" corresponds to the concept linked to the interpretation of texts in various aspects: grammatical or literal, historical, cultural and relative to the *Zeitgeist* (Spirit of the Time). The hermeneutic method was created and first used by Friedrich Ast during the first half of the 19th century (BURKE, 2004, p.45).

prudent to start with their meaning. (...) Images are made to communicate. In another sense, they reveal nothing. (BURKE, 2004, p.43).

Iconographic analyses of games are carried out in the same way as paintings or photographs, but the researcher needs to bear in mind that they can only be carried out on static images. Although at first the method of analysing a static image of a game may seem insufficient in terms of interpreting the whole game, the result that emerges shows the complete opposite: it is possible to interpret various elements of the game's context just through a printout, for example. The same goes for the game's cover, or even some concept art - which is an official drawing or painting of the specific *game* that can serve both as an advertisement and as a sketch of a specific passage in the course of the plot. In relation to this text, this method is based on analysing the images through the historical context they reproduce, not least by analysing the component elements of the different stages of the selected *games*. Thus, these games will be explored in search of particularly non-verbal (but not excluding verbal) forms of communication, recorded through the most varied resources, such as gestures, poses, looks, facial expressions, body orientations, postures, organisation and arrangement of objects, the presence of symbolic elements and objects, clothing and setting.

Representations of the hero and the Other

Every image is based on concepts of representation. It's not difficult to imagine the "game" object as a gap of suggestions not only aimed at the verisimilitude of history, but of the entire fictional context that was once dedicated exclusively to historiographical documents or even to literature.

Given that we involuntarily see *truth* as the "ontology of a world that is made up of unique identifiable objects to which we can attribute certain properties" (ANKERSMIT, 2012, p.186), it is possible to articulate creative leisure with the construction of a mentality focused on the events of history. More precisely, it is possible to appropriate concepts of the presupposition of truth from the representational means suggested by virtual game producers. Therefore, implying that *games* deal with specific events, it is safe to say that "representations are 'about' the world in the sense of 'thematicity': but they are not 'about' the world. It is true that, in a very specific context, the notion of reference can be appropriately used in relation to representation" (ANKERSMIT, 2012, p.203). Based on Ankersmit's assumption, it can be understood that video games are therefore a very influential vehicle of representations, with virtually no neutrality and full of symbolism; depending on how a context is approached by a *game*, it will influence the player in terms of their values, whether they are heroicising or derogatory.

The definition of a "hero" is full of characteristics and refers to a myth, i.e. a symbolic creation that has various values. In other words, this myth is related to that figure who has the courage to overcome his fears in order to acquire new knowledge and thus explore unknown spheres; he puts his own life at risk in order to save a cause or even a single person (MULLER, 1987, p.3). They thus tend to be adored by others, in a similar way to the superheroes in comic books or the "good guy" in an action film.

A classic model of the American fictional hero is the character Captain America, from Marvel Comics. His phenotype, in a modern conception, is what instantly brings to mind the posture of the American hero: a tall, blond, blue-eyed white man. In addition to this, in order to emphasise his role as an American hero, he dresses in the colours of his country's flag and wears only a shield, giving the impression that he is a purely defensive figure and only strikes back when he is directly attacked. His image was so popular among young Americans in the 1940s that many voluntarily joined the US Armed Forces (CHAGAS, 2008, p.140-42).

This contemporary conception of the hero is just one of the reflections of myth. The hero of Ancient History, deified and centralised for the sake of his attributes of greatness, can be exemplified with the statue of Emperor Augustus[3] , which Burke argues is a

> (...) a memorable image, [where] Augustus is depicted wearing armour, holding a spear or a banner and raising his hand as if proclaiming victory. (...) The sovereign's bare feet are not a sign of humility, as the modern viewer might think, but a means of assimilating Augustus to a god. During his long reign, the official image of Augustus remained the same, as if the emperor

[3] It is currently on display at the Gregorian Profane Museum in Rome.

> had discovered the secret of eternal youth (BURKE, 2004, p.83).

Heroicisation, therefore, arises from the glorification of a character's attributes, whether real or fictional. It's no different with the war hero: his altruistic conscience makes him risk his own life to prevent a greater disaster, such as the enemy's victory, or simply makes him use his time for good deeds, such as caring for war victims or supplying provisions for the needy. Such a perspective is narrated and publicised by photographs in the daily life of countries in conflict, and they will always be elevated as defenders of peace, and/or presented as models for other citizens to follow.

This conception is easily perceptible in Hollywood cinema. In films depicting the Second World War, the American or British man uses ethics to defeat his enemies. They fight for a "greater good", such as freedom, when they fearlessly stop the advance of their German or Japanese enemies. Most of the time, the protagonist becomes the hero, transformed into a notorious symbol of victory for his nation, or simply fades into oblivion. On some occasions, he plays the role of a "one-man army", i.e. he fights individually for the prospect of victory. Often the hero of a film doesn't even survive, in search of the fight for a cause or someone else.

In addition to these perceptions full of symbols of combat and altruism, there are also aesthetic methods of promoting heroicisation. For example, military parades and uniform displays:

> Even Frank Capra, considered one of the most prominent "makers" of the American dream, was impressed by the aestheticised Nazi ideology. In April 1942, he [and Anatole Litvak] (...) saw The Triumph of the Will, Leni Riefenstahl's now famous film. Capra was stunned: "It terrified me. My first reaction was that we were dead, we could never win that war [...] as happened with the Austrians, [...] with the countries of Europe. It was that photograph that beat them. When I saw it, I simply thought: 'How can we overcome this enormous will to fight? Surrender or you will be killed - that's what the film said (TOTA, 2000, p.24).

While "The Triumph of the Will" served as a vehicle for the notion of the hero of the German Armed Forces, at the same time there was incessant anti-capitalist and anti-communist propaganda. "Other", with a capital "O", is a reference to those who think differently from a given society (BURKE, 2004, p.153), usually the same society that heroises itself. This "Other", from the American point of view, didn't just refrain from belittling the values of its German, Japanese, Italian and other Axis sympathisers; it also applied to the culture of certain allies, such as the Soviets, due to their socialist ideology. At the same time, they heroicised themselves and belittled capitalist ideals, in a kind of ideological war through propaganda. While the notion of "correct" values is emphasised by heroicisation, its opposite occurs in the precepts of depreciation.

In short, ideological propaganda "(...) contributes to making us live another life. (...) The hysteria of the masses shows, in a certain way, the traces of this specific oppression" (CAPELATO, 1998, p.58-59). Likewise, this propaganda tends to use the most varied resources in order to publicise, for example, the cinema. If the image of the unstable strength of the Germans terrified the Americans, it was necessary to create at least one counterbalance in order to ridicule them. A notable example of satire, released at a time when the United States was not yet at war, was the feature film "The Great Dictator", which began production even before the start of the conflict.

The film was interpreted by Charles Chaplin as an ironic allusion to Adolf Hitler, played by the character Adenoid Hynkel. The atrocious dictator, thus personified by Chaplin, even made the microphones squirm in terror with his screams, as well as playing with the globe as if it were a mere inflatable ball (STEIW, 2008, p.64).

Satire is also a way of distorting the values of the Other and alluding to them as capable of leading to error. If a nation doesn't adopt democracy as the basis of its politics, it's because it's wrong - in the view of the person denouncing it - and needs to be realised in order to reshape its ideologies. In turn, while Hitler's rise was frowned upon in America, in Germany he was represented as a symbol of hope for the people whose nation had been subjugated by the Treaty of Versailles[4] (HOBSBAWM, 1995). From then on, Hitler's image as a hero grew among Nazi supporters, even if they blamed the Jews for Germany's crisis. Again in relation to the "hero" perspective, Peter Burke emphasises that:

> The grossest stereotypes are based on the simple assumption that "we" are human or civilised, while "they" are little different from animals like dogs and pigs (...). They are transformed into the exotic and detached from the self. And they can even be transformed into monsters (BURKE, 2004, p.157).

This concept of the "Other" can not only be observed in cinema or comics, but also in any other medium, through advertising (war posters, pin-ups[5]) or forms of art and entertainment, as is the case with video games, which have some historical event as their context and setting. Given that most game producers are American, it's not hard to find heroicising factors linked to the United States. This means that among their "favourite" enemies are Germans, Russians and Arabs. Electronic games depicting the Second World War, as proposed in this paper, not only emphasise the American hero, but also demoralise the values of their enemies, as in any other imagistic vehicle: it is, once again, the Germans, Japanese and former Soviet allies who are mostly selected to be part of the group of armies fighting against the ideals of freedom - which, in its context, is not a lie, but serves as a partial denunciation of a nation that is shown, almost entirely, as the only vehicle for fighting for an ideal world.

Introduction to the history of video games: Spacewar!, the forerunner

According to Skorupa (2002, p.268), science "will always be behind imagination. If the pace of its progress increases, more is expected of it," turning scientific progress into a kind of anxiety among scientists and the imagination in

[4] An imposition created by the League of Nations in the aftermath of the First World War to punish Germany for its acts of war. It consisted of the remodelling of the Germanic country: the dismantling of the empire, transforming it into a republic; 10% of the territory and population were annexed to neighbouring countries; the armed forces were restricted to 100,000 infantrymen, banning the air force, navy, armour, artillery and the use of lethal gas; nevertheless, Germany had to pay 33 billion dollars to the countries that won the war, which led the country to a peak in inflation: one dollar became worth 4.2 billion marks (JURADO, 2009, p.31-37).

[5] Realistic photographs or drawings featuring women, mostly models, in war uniforms in sensual shapes and poses. Many of these images were publicised as an encouragement to pro-Americanism during the war. The images also existed in the form of posters.

common. This need for progress led to the discovery of computing in the 20th century - the HP *200A Audio Oscillator* from 1939 can be considered one of the forerunners of computing, used to reproduce sounds. The model would be used as an audio generator for the Disney film Fantasia in 1940. That same year also saw the appearance of The Complex Number Calculator, a kind of calculator. In turn, as the Second World War progressed, technology aimed at war intelligence was researched more intensively. Machines appeared such as the German *Enigma* code generator - *and* its cryptanalysis based on Polish mathematicians; the North American *Whirlwind*, which although its design was delayed, served as a flight simulator; or the *Relay Interpolar*, a more efficient calculator based on the 1940 machine (COMPUTER HISTORY MUSEUM, 2006; SOLER, 2009, p.132-133).

Technological advances in information technology led to the creation of the first electronic games, not with the aim of providing entertainment, but to demonstrate the capabilities of the computers that were to be designed or exhibited at technology fairs. Video games as we know them[6] appeared in 1952, when language programming scientist Christopher Strachey (1916-1975) developed a virtual game that simulated checkers for the Ferranti company[7] , which ran on a Mark I computer (CAMPBELL-KELLY, 1985). In 1961, in order to demonstrate the resource capacity of the PDP-1 computer, students Steve Russell, Dan Edwards, Alan Kotok, Peter Sampson and Martin Graetz, all from the Massachusetts Institute of Technology (MIT), launched *Spacewar!* [Figure 1], initially programmed to run on a TX-0 "Tixo" computer. For its part, the PDP-1 seemed more attractive to respond to the graphic resources present in the project (GRAETZ, 1981). The topics presented on Spacewar! were as follows:

[6] I'm referring here to electronic games that simulate images on a screen. Many consider *Nim*, from 1951, presented by the electronic accessories company Ferranti in co-operation with the University of Manchester at the Berlin Festival, to be the first video game - in fact, it was an electronic game that ran on a dedicated computer, the NIMROD, but was not projected onto a screen. It was based on the operation of lights that switched on and off to simulate the positions of pieces, like the traditional matchstick game of the same name (FERRANTI COMPUTER SYSTEMS, 2015; GIBSON, 2009, p.18).

[7] Founded by Sebastian Ziani de Ferranti (1864-1930) in 1882, the company sold electrical accessories. In the 1940s, it ventured into computer technology, obtaining the co-operation of the University of Manchester in 1951. Today, the company has been dissolved into several other companies (FERRANTI COMPUTER SYSTEMS, 2015).

- It should demonstrate the computer's capabilities, using almost all of its potential;
- It should be interesting and interactive (different every time);
- It should engage the user in an attractive and enjoyable way; in other words, it should be a game (UOL JOGOS, 2017).

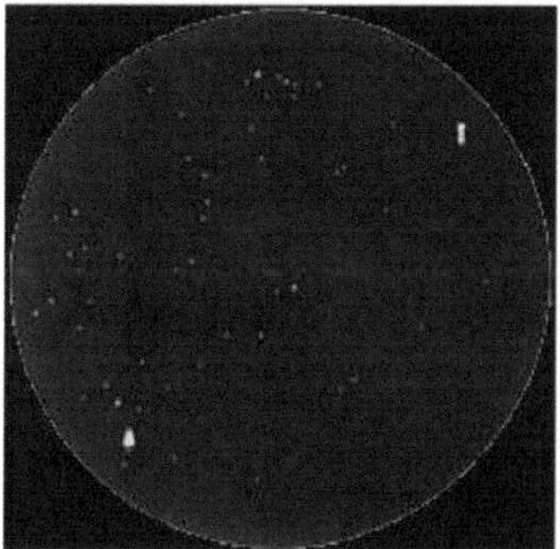

Figure 1: The first electronic game, Spacewar!, from 1961. Available at: http://zarsoft.info/info/Games/Spacewar/spacewar.gif, accessed on 10 Feb. 2017.

By saying that "it should be a game", it was understood that it followed the rules of one. Just like basketball and chess, it had its objective, rules, obstacles and improvisations. As it was a simulator featuring two ships fighting each other, the objective was clear: beat the enemy ship. The rules revolved around success within the limitations of the environment, i.e. the space of the screen; the obstacles included a star that served as a gravitational field and hindered the player's objective (GRAETZ, 1981). In addition to these difficulties, the game required the user to be skilful with its controls. Improvisations, in turn, were the means of difficulty found within all these items.

At the time of its launch, the game didn't make any money because it was a demo. Steve Russell, moving from MIT to Stanford University, presented his project to electrical engineer Nolan Bushnell. The result of this meeting was the adaptation of Spacewar! into the world's first arcade[8] , created by Nolan Bushnell himself and Ted

[8] Computers that simulate specific games, wrongly known as arcades. Arcades are actually specific places where these games are played.

Dabney and launched in 1971 (BELLIS, 2015). The arcade, distributed for the entertainment of the masses, finally turned a profit.

But Nolan Bushnell and Ted Dabney didn't hold back: the following year, decided to name their new business after entertainment technology. They christened the company Atari. Together with engineer Al Alcorn, they developed and launched a second arcade, this time introducing Pong (BELLIS, 2015).

> Legend has it that shortly after the first Pong prototype was installed at Andy Capp's Tavem in Sunnyvale, California, Atari received a phone call from the owner of the pub complaining that the machine had broken down. The engineer who had built the game, Al Alcorn, took his car and went to the pub to have a look. He discovered that the hardware worked perfectly well. It was the nature of the problem that was unexpected. The regulars had put so many 25 cent coins in the machine that it was unable to accept any more. A new sector had just been born (KRPATA, 2013, p.23).

Whether this story is true or not, the game quickly became popular. The idea was simple: two players each had to control their racket and hit the ball to their partner. Whoever scored the most points over their opponent won. It worked like a virtual version of ping-pong - hence its name.

In 1975, Pong was converted into Atari's first console, meaning that it was also marketed as a home video game. But it wasn't yet a complete console, as we know video games. It was a controller with Pong built in, which plugged directly into the television set.

In turn, the idea of selling a game for the home version was nothing new: in 1951, German-American engineer Ralph Baer had already created the first version of a console of this type. The project was rejected for fifteen years by technology companies, who considered Baer's idea to be too expensive an investment (GIBSON, 2009, p.34).

In 1956, Ralph Baer was hired by Sanders Associates Inc., a company that initially focused on air defence technology and which gradually included the production of electronic games in its interests, thanks to the engineer's research. In July 1968, Baer and the director of patents at Sanders Associates, Lou Etlinger, were formally invited to demonstrate the *Brownbox* - which had now received several adaptations from its creator and two assistants, Bill Harrison and Bill Rush - to the electronics company Magnavox. The vice-president of marketing, Gerry Martin, unlike his colleagues, was very excited about the project. He managed to convince the company's superiors to finally give in to the purchase of Baer's patent (WINTER, 2015). The result was the launch of the Magnavox Odyssey in 1972 (GIBSON, 2009, p.34), which featured 12 different generic games with no creative titles: "football", "volleyball", "hockey" - as well as virtual versions of quizzes. There was even a rifle on the console, also developed by Baer, which docked so that the player could shoot at targets on the TV screen (BIANCHIN; MITCH, p.8, 2013). Unlike Atari's Pong, which was still to be released, the Odyssey video game was a complete console with two controllers.

The second generation of video games, which lasted from 1977 to 1985, was exclusive to the Atari 2600, preceded by the Magnavox Odyssey from 1972. The visible demand for electronic games materialised both in arcades and with home gamers. In 1985, Japanese company Nintendo, which had been making card games since the 19th century, opened the third generation era with the NES, or Nintendo Entertainment System; and the following year, competitor Sega launched the Master System (BIANCHIN; MITCH, 2013, p.6-7; GIBSON, 2009, p.18).

Although the previous consoles were well received, it can be said that it was during the 1980s that games became a world reference in the electronics market, thanks to titles such as Space Invaders, Pac Man, Super Mario Bros, among others (BIANCHIN; MITCH, 2013, p.11; UOL JOGOS, 2017). For dozens of years, video games were merely assimilated into playful activities and creative leisure, as a virtual substitute for children's games and play. In turn, this assimilation was gradually overcome by titles with complex and increasingly immersive storylines, due to the resemblance to the real world that graphics engines have made possible with technological progress.

The first FPS (first-person shooter, whose perspective is "I", i.e. you literally see it from the character's eyes), the genre that is largely discussed in this text, only appeared in 1980, at a time when Pacman, Asteroids and Space Invaders were among the most popular arcade games (GIBSON, 2009). That year saw the release of Battlezone [Figure 2] for Atari, developed by Ed Rotberg (DADGUM, 2017). The game's setting is in fake 3D[9] and puts the player in the perspective of a tank commander. The game was even produced in an exclusive version for the US armoured cavalry so that tank operators could practice their marksmanship (UOL JOGOS, 2017).

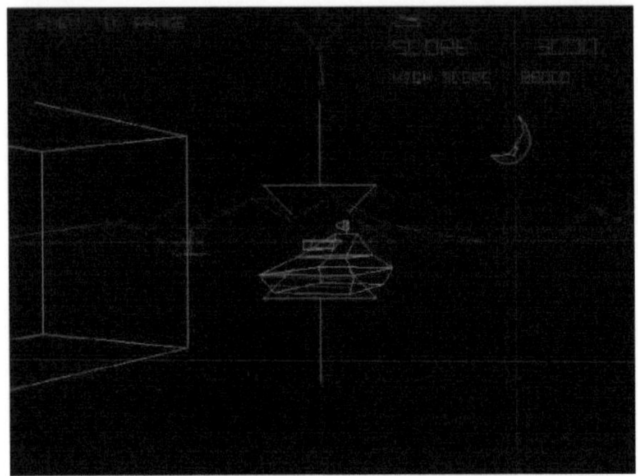

Figure 2: The first FPS, Battlezone, from 1980. Available at: <http://images.wikia.com/videogamehistory/images/7/7d/Atari_BattleZone_Screenshot.gif>, accessed on 11 Feb. 2017.

Until the 1980s or so, however, electronic game producers were not generally concerned with presenting credible and historically grounded contexts, instead favouring science fiction. The preference for fiction was due to two reasons: firstly, because of the relatively limited graphic technologies, there was no way to create in-depth backgrounds and plausible or convincing plots. This linked the production companies directly to the second reason, which was a preference for science fiction themes - until the 1980s, there was a general fascination, on a worldwide scale, with outer space and pulp fiction. It wasn't a problem, therefore, that appropriated this fascination, inserting it into most game titles as a sales strategy. Because of these aspects, it was only during the 1990s that the first electronic games truly based on

[9] "False 3D" refers to two-dimensional technologies that give the illusion of being three-dimensional, i.e. they simulate a depth perspective using only 2D mechanisms.

events from history appeared, even if it was still very difficult to get rid of the influence of fiction.

CHAPTER 2

Representations of heroes and villains: from Wolfenstein 3D to Battlefield 1942

One of the concepts that has long been debated among historians is the notion of "veracity". This concept was gradually deconstructed by historians over the course of the 20th century, since until then, for the positivist followers of Ranke, cultural history seemed to be just an inexact alternative way of reading history (BURKE, 2004, p.17). Instead of "truthfulness", history was subject to "representativeness". Since truth can be understood as the

> (...) ontology of a world that is composed of unique identifiable objects, to which we can attribute certain properties (...), representations are 'about' the world in the sense of "temacity": but they are not "about" the world. It is true that, in a very specific context, the notion of reference can be appropriately used in relation to representation (ANKERSMIT, 2012, p.186-203).

If an object serves as a "reference" for history, then all sources, primary or secondary, carry representations of their relative times and places. Therefore, books, films, photographs and works of art are nothing more than accounts of a historical context - but they will never convey history as a herald of truth.

The same goes for electronic games that seek to represent events in history. The number of titles is huge, with different genres, platforms and release dates.

Wolfenstein 3D (1992)

In the 1990s, the first video games to deal with the Second World War were presented in the FPS style. The first of its kind was Wolfenstein 3D (1992), by id Software, which originally ran on the MS DOS platform and was divided into three chapters. In them, the player controls American spy William "B.J." Blazkowicz, a prisoner in the fictional German castle *Wolfenstein, and* seeks his way out by fighting various Nazi soldiers, including Hitler in robotic armour.

Analysing the image of the original North American promotional poster for Wolfenstein 3D can help us understand some of the representations conveyed by the game:

Figura 3: Cover of Wolfenstein 3D, from 1992. Available at: <http://cidadegamer.com.br/wp-content/uploads/2012/07/wolf3d-capa-cover.jpg>, accessed on 11 Feb. 2017.

An iconological reading of the image shows the American soldier in the foreground, whose appearance is very similar to the style of Rambo[10] : he is shirtless, exposing his muscles; he is wearing boots and a red bandana (although not on his forehead, but on his wrist). The rifle he carries - totally fictitious and timeless - fires randomly into the air; at the same time, his German enemy is hit and disarmed, so that his anachronistic M16[11] fires upwards. A third soldier runs towards them carrying an

[10] Feature film from 1982. Rambo (Sylvester Stallone) is a Vietnam veteran unjustly imprisoned by Sheriff Will Teasle (CINE PLAYERS, 2017).

[11] Semi-automatic rifle that holds 5.56 x 45mm NATO ammunition, used as the primary weapon of the US infantry from 1967 onwards, still occasionally used. It fires 800 to 900 rounds per minute, depending on the model (WORLD GUNS, 2017).

MP40[12] , which is the only weapon in the image that is faithful to the context of the Second World War.

In terms of the figures' facial expressions, it can be seen that Blazkowicz is totally focused on his blow, while his enemy has a melancholic expression of pain. His body posture, as a result of the blow received, shows that he, unable to defend himself, has been completely subdued and is about to hit the ground. From an iconographic point of view, there are contextual elements that are quite biased towards the figure. Starting with some aspects relating to the hero depicted. In the way he dresses, he carries the colours of the US flag in the blue of his trousers and the red of his bandana. The personification of the flag, in the form of a soldier striking the enemy, may be an attempt to present the American country as superior to the threat, so that a simple action is enough to subdue it. In other words, the two figures in the foreground may represent the United States and Nazi Germany.

What's more, Blazkowicz is placed in the centre of the image when he knocks him down. Probably so as not to use gratuitous violence in the image, even though this is a shooting game, the scene shows a confrontation without shooting the opponent, even though the three characters use firearms (besides, in the game itself, there is no option to hit them directly). However, the weapon used by the protagonist is proportional to the size of his body, making the hero a true exterminator of the Nazi threat.

Another message we can extract from the game's cover is the purpose of the *game*'s content - the theme of "action", in a very literal sense. You can see the unusual behaviour of the German soldier in the background, who runs towards the enemy instead of surrendering with his weapon, while the enemy is distracted by the blow against the German. This idea refers to the interaction of the game, which implies that it is only taken up by moments of action, and never of idleness. In other words, it shows that the enemy is not tactical and that the protagonist must defend himself against relentless waves of Germans.

---

[12] Short for *Maschinenpistole 40*, it served as the *Wehrmacht*'s standard weapon from 1939 to 1945. With a calibre of 9x19 mm, it fired 500 rounds per minute (LUDEKE, 2011, p. 11).

The impact of this image for the North American public of the early 1990s is the use of physical strength, stereotyped by the agent's excessive muscles. Nevertheless, it expresses freedom, a sentiment much emphasised by the nation, as the hero of the game wears no shirt or uniform, while the Germans are duly uniformed in Heer uniforms[13] . The colours of Blazkowicz's clothes combine with his sense of freedom, making him a threat to the rigid Nazi discipline, which is, above all, referred to in this video game as an oppressor of free will. In the content of the game, this oppression is literal, as it takes place partly in the prisons of Wolfenstein's castle.

The notion of freedom, combined with the political precepts of American democracy, has long been defended by American morality:

> (...) [The thought of freedom] can be better understood if we analyse some of its most important elements, which took shape in the United States mainly from the first half of the 20th century. One of them is democracy, which has always been associated with American heroes and, in particular, with the ideas [sic] of freedom, individual rights and independence. Democracy, freedom and individual rights were guaranteed for all the American people, overcoming differences of class, creed and race (TOTA, 2000, p.19).

In this way, the Americans were presented as the representatives of freedom and democracy, while the Other was a notion that referred to error, rather than an undesirable option, because it meant a totalitarian affront to American values. As one of the first figures in a game to convey these values, Blazkowicz served as an inspiration for many other characters who would come to be associated with American heroism.

Medal of Honor (1999)

Over the next few years, the heroicisation of American characters in video games became evident and remained the standard, a fact that shouldn't cause any surprise, given that all the renowned games were produced by US companies. Seven years after the success of Wolfenstein 3D, the FPS Medal of Honor (1999) was released for the Playstation platform, produced by Dreamworks Interactive and distributed by Electronic Arts. The game and its sequels were recognised by Guinness World Records

[13] Part of the German Armed Forces that corresponds to the army.

2009: Games as the most successful World War II video game series: "To date, more than 31 million copies of Medal of Honor have been sold since the release of the first game in 1999" (SHOEMAKER, 2009, p. 48).

Although it was a successful series in a similar way to its predecessor Wolfenstein 3D, the first Medal of Honor brought with it very different elements that had been known to gamers until then. The first elements of these differences, in contrast to id Software's 1992 game, could be seen on its original North American cover [Figure 4]

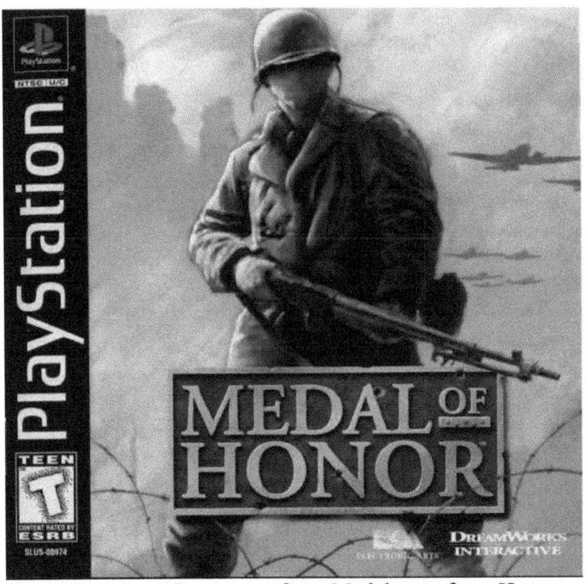

Figura 4: Cover of Medal of Honor (1999). Available at: < http://www.mobygames.com/images/covers/l/15522-medal-of-honor-playstation-front-cover.jpg >, accessed on 12 Feb. 2017.

The cover of Figure 4 shows the game's protagonist, Lieutenant James Steven "Jimmy" Patterson, an *Airborne* soldier[1]. We notice that the setting is geographically unrecognisable, although it probably refers to the first missions of the game, in the vicinity of Normandy, France. However, the devastation in the background is undeniable: there is an excess of smoke and dust, barbed wires and the silhouettes of aeroplanes flying overhead - probably C-47 Dakota models [14][15], standard transport machines for Anglo-American paratroopers during the war[16]. The orange colour of the scenery also suggests a "hellish" atmosphere, taking the setting to be one destroyed by fire. In turn, the only figure that stands out and is highlighted in colour from the rest of the monochrome setting is the American character.

Although Patterson is at the centre of the picture, he is not presented emphatically (again, if we compare it to the then standard Blazkowicz-style emphasis). His figure is thoughtful: on the cover of Medal of Honor, Patterson is presented in a very reflective manner. His pose is typical of a soldier: his legs ajar are almost bent and he holds his gun carefully, making him succinctly crouch, aim and fire - a pose that emphasises his high discipline as a military man.

The weapon he is holding is a BAR[17]. This light machine gun, classified as an LMG (light machine gun), was used in the war as a support weapon. The function of LMGs is to suppress fire and help fellow soldiers move during bursts, forcing the enemy to take cover. Even though he has a great collective function, however, the character in the game is alone, both in the game itself and on the cover. This harks back to the central idea of Medal of Honor, how the protagonist's journey through war is crucial to the fall of Nazi Germany. His gun gives him a pose of grandeur, as if he were using it like any other assault weapon. This means that, even though he demonstrates a disciplined and more realistic pose (unlike the common exaggerated poses of the hero), Patterson reveals himself to be a true "one-man army": jargon known to refer to heroic legends in war stories.

[14] Anglo-American paramilitary force. In Figure 4, however, the uniform is a simple allusion and does not follow any real pattern of American war uniforms. There is also no coat of arms or insignia of any kind.

[15] A military version of the Douglas DC-3 aeroplane, the C-47 Dakota was widely manufactured by the United States from 1940 onwards. It reached 370 km/h and could carry up to 28 soldiers or three tonnes of equipment (WARBIRD ALLEY, 2017).

[16] We can rule out the possibility that the image refers to German transport planes, since the angle of their wings would be perceptibly sharper. Speculating that these were German bombers would also be a mistake, given that there were no large-scale German bombing raids on German-occupied France in 1944, according to the context in which the image is presented.

[17] Browning Automatic Rifle, 7.62mm calibre light machine gun. It holds 20 projectiles per cartridge and fires 350 to 500 shots per minute, depending on the model. It has greater stability when fired using its bipod (LÚDEKE, 2011, p.37).

The "one-man army" is a reference to those soldiers in war who are super-efficient and fulfil their objectives with determination and self-confidence. These characters are often emphasised in action films, such as Stallone's own Rambo, and in films of the genre, such as those starring Jean Claude Van Damme or Arnold Schwarzenegger during the 1980s and 1990s. In Medal of Honor, Patterson fulfils this role, as during the game, for example, he destroys a heavy water plant[18] and another V-2 missile plant [19][20] .

For his part, although Patterson is depicted as an *Airborne* soldier on the *game*'s cover, he is no mere soldier - but an OSS20 spy. Curiously, he's depicted as an ordinary combatant even though he's not one. It's true that part of the first and fourth missions place the player in fairly open combat scenarios, respectively in the village of Dubuisson, France, and possibly - given that the game only presents it as a location on the Siegfried Line[21] - in the forest of Hurtgen, Germany.

The first mission in the game consists of a simple objective: to retrieve the secret documents from a US plane that was shot down near Dubuisson. The date of this mission was not chosen at random by the producers: 12 June, just six days after D-Day (this event will be duly presented later in this text). Along the way, Patterson fights both *Wehrmacht* light infantrymen[22] and *Gestapo* agents[23] and their trained dogs. After recovering the important documents, the agent is assigned to more difficult missions, many of which have *stealth* elements.

The aim of the second mission, for example, is to neutralise the threat posed

---

[18] Heavy water is a substance derived from deuterium and used in nuclear reactors. The Germans developed their heavy water research emphatically until 1943, when the plant in Norway was sabotaged by the Allies in conjunction with the Norwegian resistance (ROMANA, 2010, p.258-261; SVITRAS, 2017).

[19] The V-2, or *Peenemunde A-4*, were the first mass-produced liquid propellant rockets used by the Germans in 1944 and 1945, based on designs created by aerospace engineer Wernher von Braun. Their main targets were France and England. The V-2 was the precursor model to the space rockets used in the Cold War (ROMANA, 2010, p. 282-307).

[20] *Office of Strategic Services,* or "Strategic Services Agency", was the formation of the US secret service responsible for intelligence in the Second World War (OSSSOCIETY, 2017).

[21] German defence line made up of forts and *bunkers* in the western part of the country (VITORIA, 2009, p.35-47).

[22] Germany's armed forces, divided into three: the *Heer* (army), the *Kriegsmarine* (navy) and the *Luftwaffe* (air force).

[23] Abbreviation for *Geheime Staatspolizei*, or "Secret State Police", espionage formation of the *Reichssicherheitshauptamt*, originally headed by Reinhard Heydrich (*Reich* Central Security Office) with unquestioned powers of arrest (BUTLER, 2004, p.56).

by the Greta railcannon[24] , then an obstacle to the approach of Allied ships off the coast of Normandy. To get to the weapon, the protagonist disguises himself as a Wehrmacht captain and carries false identification documents into a railway station under Nazi control. The mission, as the game itself tells you before it begins, takes place on 15 July 1944.

The way the Germans approach the American in disguise is revealing. The speech of the Gestapo agents scattered around the train station (and also at later moments in the game, which occur in a similar way, but with soldiers from other military functions and ranks) is quite formal, even when referring to what they believe to be a *Wehrmacht* captain - which is curious given the fact that there has been a certain rivalry between the two military organisations, even under the same ideological banner[25] . When they encounter these agents, they ask the controlled character the following questions, more or less at random:

- Sir, are you lost?
- Are you new here, sir?
- Sir, I need to see some identification.
- May I see your papers, please?
- *You don't have the proper identification.*
- *I'm sorry sir, but I can 7 letyou in.*
- Your papers are in order.
- Sir, the papers are not in order.
- Forgive me, sir.
- What unit are you from?

[24] Railcannons were large 80 cm calibre cannons that travelled along railway tracks. The fictional Greta model was based on the German Dora and Gustav, both built in 1937. The initial purpose of these guns was to lay siege to Alsace via the fortified Maginot Line (LÚDEKE, 2011, p.154).

[25] The rivalry began with friction between Hermann Goring, co-founder of the Gestapo himself (1933), but an energetic representative of the Wehrmacht, and Heinrich Himmler, who was then chief of police in Munich and an increasingly influential veteran within the SS. Both thought they were suitable for the job, but it was Himmler who ended up being appointed head of the secret police in 1936. With the powerful police under his control, Himmler went on to become the man most responsible for the Holocaust (1941-1945) (BUTLER, 2004, p.27-37).

- Sorry sir, have a good night.[26]

These words are "more or less random" because they depend on the situation. The German soldier may ask to see the documents, respond to being shown the documents, or even indicate suspicion about the American's true identity.

When they ask the protagonist to present his documents, they always do so in English, with an unmistakable German accent. For example, in words that end with er, the speaker pronounces a, according to the official German language. Thus, order is pronounced as orda. And although the game's accessible files indicate that Patterson knows German, at no point does he respond to his suspicious enemies.

However, the fact that the Germans in the game communicate only in English is probably intended to make it easier for the player to understand what they are asking for, enquiring about or informing him about; but it could also indicate how Patterson understands them, given that he knows German. In other words, he understands his enemies as easily as he understands English, albeit with an accent - perhaps due to his lack of familiarity with the Germanic language.

The enemies' interaction with the character/player, however, is not only verbal. Many of them, on spotting the fake officer, quickly greet him with an emphatic Sieg Heil [Figure 5].

[26] In Portuguese, respectively, the sentences can be understood as: "Are you lost? / Are you new here, sir? / Sir, I need to see some certification. / May I see your documents, please? / You don't have the proper identification. / I'm sorry, sir, but I can't let you in. / Your papers are in order. / Forgive me, sir. / What unit are you from? / Excuse me, sir, have a good evening."

Figure 5: Gestapo agent gives a Nazi salute. Image available at: <http://i1137.photobucket.com/albums/n513/mecha-neko/MedalOfHonor/MedalOfHonor_PSX_png_26.png>, accessed 13 Feb. 2017.

The Sieg Heil was a greeting given by Nazi sympathisers, as suggested by the agent's pose in Figure 5: body erect, right arm raised at around fifty to seventy degrees - although, in this image, instead of extending his right arm, the soldier greets with his left arm, possibly due to some oversight in the programming. The salute was used from the 1920s onwards as an exclusive exaltation of the National Socialist German Labour Party[27] . *Heil* means health to the Germans - not just physical, but spiritual. After Hitler was appointed *Führer* in 1933, the greeting changed to *Heil Hitler* (save *Hitler*). From now on, at pro-Nazi marches and Hitler's speeches, the sympathising public shouted "*Heil* //ú/er/", and among the military of the *Third Reich*, the salute became a salute. However, as a direct allusion to Nazism, the greeting ceased to be legal after the war until today in several countries (EVANS, 2017).

In Medal of Honor, this salute, when performed by Gestapo agents, is accompanied by lines such as "Sieg Heil!", "Hello!" and "Captain!", but never in

[27] From the original *Nationalsozialistische Deutsche Arbeiterpartei*, abbreviated to "Nazi", it was created in 1919 by sports journalist Karl Harrer and railway mechanic Anton Drexler. Its main ideological principles were anti-Semitism and anti-communism (RYBACK, 2009, p.55-56).

reference to Hitler, although the scenery is entirely adorned with flags and coats of arms with swastikas .[28]

Throughout the game, we notice that although Patterson is disguised as a *Wehrmacht* captain, when he presents his documents - as seen in Figure 5 - the colour of the uniform on his arm is navy blue, instead of the army's olive green. But when he selects the pistol, his uniform shows the appropriate colour. This could be a bug[29] related to the following mission, since Patterson is disguised as a Kriegsmarine officer, which corresponds to the navy blue uniform. But when in this mission as a naval officer the player swaps his passport for his pistol, he is once again dressed in olive-coloured clothing. The mistake was probably noticed by the producers; but, remembering that in the Playstation 1 generation, most games' memory had to fit on just one CD, it's likely that caring about the respective uniform colours in their contexts would have required a lot of unnecessary memory, as well as being a practically unnoticeable aspect in its day.

Finally, in its context, Medal of Honor continued in a similar vein to those presented above until its last mission, alternating between moments of shooting and espionage and leading the player to sabotage important machines for the Germans. With an arsenal of weapons faithful to the combat and a striking soundtrack[30] , it was a game that permeated the memory of gamers in the 1990s.

Medal of Honor: Underground (2000)

The direct sequel to Medal of Honor is also a Playstation 1 classic. Released in 2000, also by Dreamworks and the new part of Electronic Arts, EA, under the subtitle Underground, the title presented novelties not only in its context, but also in its mechanics. While the first game presented an almost absolutely static scenario, in terms of the dynamics of enemy movements, now the player had to face enemy tanks,

[28] References to Nazism have not always been precise when it comes to the use of the swastika in games about the Second World War. Especially since the 2000s, many games have been produced without alluding to Nazism in the flags displayed in the game itself, i.e. the swastika has been replaced by other coats of arms or symbols of Germany. These changes are visible, for example, in the games Battlefield 1942 (2002), Medal of Honor: European Assault (2005) and Sniper Elite: V2 (2012).

[29] A term used in computer science to designate a defect.

[30] The soundtrack, orchestrated by composer Michael Giachinno, can be seen at the following link: <https://www.youtube.com/watch?v=C3dYiawUXJA>, accessed 13 Feb. 2017.

semi-laggarts and motorbikes on the move, watch out for bombing raids from low-flying planes and even count on a few allies. Compared to the first game, Medal of Honor: Underground was more difficult.

Most of the game takes place before the first title: from May 1942 to June 1944. The first and last missions of the game take place in Nazi-occupied France[31] . In its context, one of the most emphatic anti-Nazi organisations was the French Resistance, directly supported by General De Gaulle, who was in exile in London. In 1944, with France already vacated through Allied interference, De Gaulle was elected president of the Provisional Government of the French Republic, in opposition to the collaborationist Phillipe Pétain. At first, the Resistance operated only by disseminating pamphlets and other ways of spreading anti-Nazism, but as it grew, it organised major armed operations and sabotage (CARDONA, 2009, p.7-33; POLLAK, 1992, p.205).

In Medal of Honor: Underground, the player controls a female member of this resistance: Manon Batiste. As the character progresses through her missions in the game, she also becomes a member of the OSS. While in the first game in the series no real combat character was referenced, this time the protagonist was an allusion to Helène Deschamps, a figure who fought against the Nazis in occupied France, and who even co-operated in the production of the game as a consultant (SHOEMAKER, 2009, p.49). From a military family, Deschamps began his activities in the Resistance in 1940. She joined the militia, the collaborationist army, and destroyed documents ordering the execution of Jews and members of the French Resistance. She was almost executed by another resistance group when they discovered her forged Nazi documents, which led to her leaving the resistance to serve as an OSS informer (MARTIN, 2006).

Deschamps' virtual personification, Manon, serves as the female version of the "one-man army", although she does have a few allies during the course of the game.

[31] France was occupied by Germany from 10 to 22 June 1940. The siege was broken in the north after the German armed forces crossed the Ardennes forest into Belgium in order to avoid the fortifications of the Maginot Line. In the same year, the collaborationist Philippe Pétain encouraged the French population to help the occupiers, which resulted in a massive recruitment of Frenchmen into the Wehrmacht (VÁZQUEZ, 2009, p.99-124).

Even so, her role remains as an independent combatant, since her allies don't make much difference in practice: many of them are part of the game's missions and must be rescued by Manon or simply accompany her to some fatal destination. Random figures, on very rare occasions, are seen fighting the Germans, although they are quickly neutralised by enemy fire. The North American cover of the game [Figure 6] is designed to present the protagonist as if she were posing for a photo, so that the image gives the impression of having been reproduced by a second figure in the company of Manon.

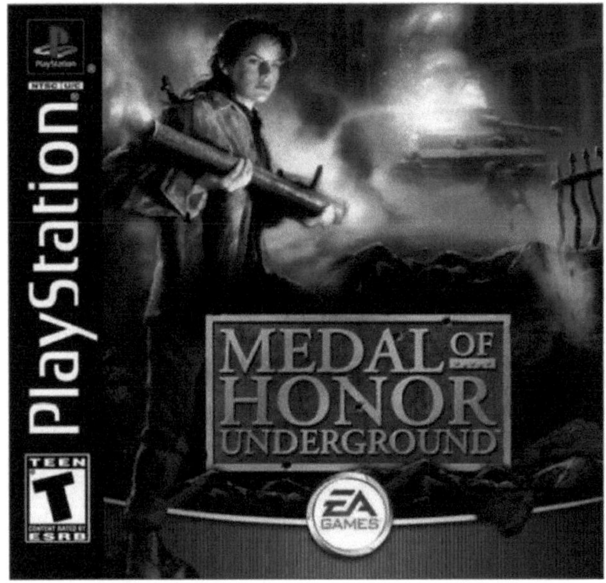

Figure 6: Cover of Medal of Honor: Underground, 2000. Image available at: <http://4.bp.blogspot.com/-RUy1sFw6QE4/TWJ4s7KMaYI/AAAAAAAACYo/eWKF0NuRC-E/s1600/mohu.jpg>, accessed 1 March 2017.

The character's outfit does not allude to any uniform of the French Armed Forces, since the Resistance didn't wear one either - although the olive green colour gives a military meaning to her role as a combatant. Her outfit matches her lack of vanity usually associated with female figures: there are no adornments or make-up on her face, nor any traces of nail polish on her nails; although her image is made up of beautiful feminine features - apart from her long hair and well-drawn eyebrows - the elements of the image allude to the fact that she is an active and fearless fighter.

Although during the war many women took part in direct combat against the invading armies, most were employed in the manufacture of weapons or war machines in mass-production factories or as nurses, especially in countries that were not geographically threatened by the Germans. In the United States, for example,

> [...] female participation was especially important in the defence industries. Between 1940 and 1944, the number of women working in manufacturing increased by 141 per cent. In Detroit in 1943, up to 91 per cent of the new jobs created in 185 war industries were filled by women. More than 10 per cent of the workers in the shipbuilding industry were women. Most of these jobs were conditional on the "blue ticket", as women knew they would be fired when the men returned from the war (WILLMOT, 2008, p.125).

On the other hand, when they were deployed to fight within the invaded countries, they were not part of the formal army (with the exception of some nations like the Soviet Union, for example), but were essential in forming the resistance. In France, "there wasn't a man left. It was the women who started the Resistance. Women didn't have the right to vote, they didn't have bank accounts, they didn't have jobs. But women were able to resist" (TILLION, apud CUNHA, 2011).

Manon, therefore, differs from the traditional image of the female figure in the Second World War in that she is not represented as a bureaucrat, nurse or pin-up model. In turn, she only becomes an officer due to her experience in the conflicts themselves - which, in terms of verisimilitude, is quite unlikely, given that in the first part of her first mission, she neutralises dozens of collaborationists armed only with a pistol and Molotov cocktails; In turn, still in Figure 6, we see her carrying a Panzerfaust[32] in her arms - which is not an anachronistic error if we allude to the fifth and sixth missions, which also take place in France, but in 1944. The same weapon is also used in the first mission, which takes place in 1942. There is a slight anachronism here. The Panzerfaust was only used for the first time in 1943 against Soviet tanks and

[32] A light, disposable anti-tank weapon (one shot) that was easy to handle and very effective even against heavy tanks, with little chance of failure. They were manufactured in 30 klein (small), 30, 60, 100 and 150 models, which differed only in the distance the projectile could travel (LÚDEKE, 2011, p.15).

was produced on a large scale in 1944 (WORLD GUNS, 2017). On its back, you can see the barrel of an MP40. In other words, both the weapons he is carrying are German, stolen or smuggled.

The cover image probably alludes to the first, fifth or sixth mission, given that it's an urban environment in ruins (the debris to the left and right of the EA Games logo is identical, as if pasted and copied without much change). The only missions that take place in an urban setting in the game are in Paris. Manon is in front of a Panzer[33] , destroyed by a frontal detonation of its Panzerfaust, which emits smoke. A fleeing German soldier can also be seen near the carcass of the tank. Although it was difficult for battle tanks to be destroyed once they were hit in the front, the Panzerfaust had a special feature: a hollow charge projectile.

> The hollow-charge projectile contains a high-explosive charge with a profiled copper jacket at the front and an aerodynamic "windscreen" to give it the necessary ballistic shape. When the base fuze operates, the copper jacket is deformed when it hits the target to form a powerful jet from the charge that penetrates the target's armour and launches a stream of flames and hot gas into the tank (MERETSKOV, 2014).

The Panzer Type III SDKZF 141 model Ausf.E was the tank most used in the invasion of France (BURSTEIN, 2009, p.25; LÚDEKE, 2011, p.70). In turn, the tank shell in the cover illustration alludes to a Panzer Tiger, also known as the Panzer VI (the main differences[34] between the two models on the cover are the shape of the cannon and the angle of the armour on the tracks). The Tiger model was first used in 1942 in the African campaign, and later on the eastern front, manufactured precisely because of the results obtained in the French campaign from the obsolete Panzer III. While the latter weighed 22 tonnes, reached 40 km per hour and used a 75 mm cannon and a 7.92 mm machine gun (ABRIL COLEÇÕES, 2010, p.117); the Tiger, on the other hand, weighed 60 tonnes, travelled at a maximum speed of 39 km per hour and was armed with an 8.8 cm cannon and two 7.92 mm machine guns. Among the Allied armies, the Tiger was a cause for concern: in 1944, a single Panzer VI Tiger was

---

[33] "Tank" in German. In turn, the word *Panzer* was used worldwide to refer to German tanks. In some German dialects, *Panzer* means "paunchy".

[34] It was my colleague Rodrigo Gomes who first noticed the tank model in the picture.

responsible for destroying 25 Allied tanks advancing on the German defence lines (LÚDEKE, 2011, p.74). Ironically, however, Manon doesn't come across any Panzer VIs in the game's content. The only appearance of the tank is in the seventh mission (1944), already destroyed (MEDAL OF HONOR WIKI, 2017).

In addition to the anachronisms present in the game, one of the most improbable aspects is the armour on the enemy tanks. Although the player is in possession of a Panzerfaust in the first mission, it is possible to destroy the Panzers with absolutely any weapon. No machine-gun projectile is capable of destroying a tank, unless its engine is exposed at the rear; even shots from a Walther P38[35] can put an end to the Panzers, even if they deal minimal damage.

Implausible and impossible aspects like this are constantly emphasised throughout the game - remembering that Manon is always outnumbered, as well as having an inferior arsenal and training - referring to the greatness of the skills attributed to her. At the same time, this greatness tends to demean the Nazi soldiers in terms of ability, so that they appear in the game as inferior in armed conflict, as well as being presented as lacking sufficient intelligence to carry out a combat strategy against Manon.

Battlefield 1942 (2002)

In 2002, for the first time in the history of video games, it became possible to play as a soldier in the service of the Axis. The Battlefield series, produced by Dice and distributed by EA, allowed the player to experience both sides of the fronts in their respective contexts. The most recent title, Battlefield 1 (2016), presented this experience in the settings of the First World War (1914-1918); the first game in the franchise, on the other hand, was set in the context of the Second World War.

The game, called Battlefield 1942, was designed to be played in online multiplayer mode[36] (although it was also possible to play single player, i.e. with bots[37] in place of other players). The game simulates more than 20 World War II scenarios

[35] A cheap and easy-to-use pistol used by the German military from 1938 onwards (LÚDEKE, 2011, p.10).

[36] Game mode via internet connection, where you play with other people online.

[37] In FPS, bots are artificial intelligence combatants that simulate the actions of players.

and doesn't follow a scripted sequence, meaning that each game differs from the other due to the freedom of the scenarios. In them, the player can act as an infantryman, drive a tank, fly an aeroplane, etc. - all without following a path predefined by the game.

As already mentioned, you can also fight on either side of the battle. Depending on the battle scenario, you can play as an American, Russian or British fighter, but also as a German or Japanese (the Italians are excluded in this version[38] of Battlefield 1942). Offering the possibility of playing as an Axis soldier was a necessity for the producer in order for their title to be well-designed in one respect: the online game. To make it possible to play, it was necessary to have a "team versus team" mode.

Along with the possibility of playing as a soldier from Nazi Germany, however, came the concern to omit symbols related to the regime. There are no swastikas in the game, not even on the flags. Germany is referred to as the flag in Figure 7:

Figura 7: Flag representing the Axis in Battlefield 1942. Image available at: <http://images.wikia.com/battlefield/images/f/f7/Flag_Germany_1933.png>, accessed 02 Mar. 2017.

This version of the flag is an allusion to the symbol of the Reichskriegsflagge, the Reich's war flag, which in turn was used more ceremonially. The difference between the game version [Figure 7] and the original is in the symbol in the centre: instead of the Germanic cross of malta, the producers inserted a Balkenkreuz, which was used as a generic Wehrmacht identification symbol.

[38] In addition to the game's official expansion, which makes the Italian army playable (The Road to Rome, 2003), Battlefield 1942 can be modified with free online content. Forgotten Hope, for example, is a modification that transforms the game into a more accurate experience in terms of scenarios, arsenals, nations, etc. To find out more, see <http://forgottenhope.warumdarum.de/about.php?>.

Probably fearing that the game could partially represent a defence of Nazism, the producers decided to represent Germany in a more military than ideological way. Thus, when playing with the German army, the player has the impression that he is controlling a non-ideological soldier, sent to the battlefront only to fulfil his role as a soldier, which in this case boils down to following orders and conquering important points in the scenarios presented.

The presentation of the Japanese Empire was not unequal: instead of being represented with the flag of the Imperial Army, the nation was alluded to with the Japanese national flag, with a white background and a red sphere in the centre. The nations belonging to the Allies, on the other hand, are shown with their respective flags (the United States, Great Britain and the Soviet Union).

In addition to the omission of symbols, the game also contains a number of errors, mainly in relation to the anachronism of arsenals. For example, the use of the STG

44[39] in battles at the beginning of the war. This assault rifle was only manufactured in 1944. But the mistakes go further: when playing with the Japanese, for example, you can handle only German weapons, such as the STG 44, the K-98 carbine, the Walther P38 pistol, the Panzerschrek anti-tank gun and the MP18 submachine gun. With the Soviet army, the weapons available are presented in a similar way: they have the Lee-Enfield No.4 rifle, the BAR light machine gun, the Bazooka anti-tank gun, the Colt pistol and, again, the German MP18 submachine gun. These weapons featured in the Japanese and Soviet nations are all "reused" from the American, British and German classes. The Soviets and Japanese seem to be excluded by the game's producers, even though they take part in the most important battles. For example, in the game, the Soviets don't even have the Red Army's standard infantry submachine gun, the PPSh[40]

[39] Short for Sturmgewehr 44, the first assault rifle in history, created in 1944. It had 30 rounds per magazine and fired 500 rounds per minute. It served as a model for several other weapons of this type, such as the Russian AK 47 (LÚDEKE, 2011, p.12).

[40] Soviet submachine gun that fired 800 rounds per minute and held a magazine of 35 or 71 projectiles. It was directly based on the Finnish Suomi, considered the best submachine gun of the Second World War (ABRIL COLEÇÕES, 2010, p.152; LÚDEKE, 2011, p.28).

; perhaps the only coherence in the arsenal of these two nations is in the machinery: the planes, tanks and motorised artillery are consistent with their respective armed forces.

Bearing in mind that this is a relatively old game, it's important to remember that graphics engines in 2002 could cost Battlefield 1942 to be more historically accurate - again, later on, the modifications available online would satisfy the most demanding players. The strongest feature of Battlefield 1942, at the time of its release, was the relative freedom it allowed the player to explore the scenarios and create their own strategy. This way, they weren't forced to follow the same path throughout the game, defining the methods by which they and their team could outwit their enemies.

CHAPTER 3

Representations of the Alliance and the Axis in Call of Duty titles

The classic franchise

After the launch of electronic game series such as Medal of Honor and Battlefield, both from EA, a major competitor emerged: Call of Duty, distributed by Activision and divided to this day between producers Infinity Ward, Treyarch and Sledgehammer Games. Winner of several awards[41] , the first title was released in 2003 for PC[42] and was only produced for video games the following year, with parallel stories.

At first, the franchise seemed to be dedicated only to the confrontation between 1939 and 1945, but left aside all historical attributes to dedicate itself to futuristic themes, which displeased fans and began to decline in sales numbers - as in the then most recent title, *Infinite Warfare*, from 2016 (LIPPE, 2016). In turn, the "golden age" of *Call of Duty* seemed to last for many years, including the *Modern Warfare* trilogy (2007-2011), which even though it moved away from the battles of the Second World War to focus on present-day combat - such as in the Middle East - it pleased even the most demanding fans. For their part, the first *Call of Duty games* were contextualised in the fight against Nazism, trying to represent important battles on the European stage. In the first two *games*, the player controlled characters on different *fronts*: in Eastern and later Western Europe, with the Soviet army; in North Africa and western France, with the British; and to the north, also in France, with US soldiers. The third title in the series differed from the previous ones in that it presented only the viewpoint of the Americans at the front, as well as the almost unnoticed participation

[41] The first title in the series won several awards from the Academy of Interactive Arts and Sciences: *Call of Duty 4: Modern Warfare* was voted Best Action Game of the Year, Console Game of the Year and Outstanding Achievement in Online Games in 2008; 2006's *Call of Duty 2* won Best Character Development/Story titles; *Call of Duty 3* was honoured for Best Sound Production in 2007. In addition, it was awarded Best Release of the Year by BAFTA in 2004 (SHOEMAKER, 2009, p.47).

[42] The first *Call of Duty* was later released for *Playstation 3* and *Xbox 360* in 2009.

of French and Polish Resistance soldiers. In 2008, with the title *World at War* - which was the fifth game in the franchise, released the year after the first *Modern Warfare* - the player experienced two distant *fronts*: Eastern Europe, with a Soviet soldier, and the Pacific, with an American .[43]

Among the battles between the Allies and the Axis, the games in the franchise feature the battles of D-Day, Stalingrad, Peleliu, Okinawa, Berlin, El Alamein, Tobruk, among others. Before turning these events into games, the production team did a lot of historical research: to create the setting for *Call of Duty 2,* for example, "the game's artists travelled to North Africa and Normandy and came back with 10,000 photographs, videos and audio recordings" (SHOEMAKER, 2009, p.47).

Although this routine of historical research has been put aside in favour of a futuristic context in the franchise's titles, the future of *Call of Duty* is currently uncertain. With the success of EA's competitor, *Battlefield 1*, the tendency is for Activision to try to recapture some of the nostalgia provided by the conflicts of yesteryear, in order to repair the damage of its gradual decline.

The US soldiers

In 2003, EA, which had practically dominated game franchises that depicted the Second World War, such as *Medal of Honor* and *Battlefield*, gained a competitor. The first *Call of Duty* was launched.

In its context, with the exception of the game's first mission, all the episodes take place in Nazi Europe. This first mission shows part of a training session at a military base in Georgia, USA, and serves as a prelude to familiarising the player with commands such as jumping, crouching, aiming and firing. The American protagonist is Private Martin, a member of the 506th Parachute Infantry Regiment, assigned to the 101st Airborne Division[44] . This division was essential for the execution of Operation Overlord: D-Day.

Operation Overlord consisted of applying a bridgehead across Normandy

---

[43] In the same game, in addition to the main character, Private Miller, the player also experiences the sailor Petty Locke in the "Black Cats" mission.

[44] This information is provided the moment the game is loaded.

beach, in the north of France, in order to open the way for the Allies in Europe. Known as the largest amphibious assault in history (JORGENSEN, 2007, p. 231), it involved approximately 155,000 Allies led by General D. Eisenhower. They landed with 4,126 transport boats, supported by more than 1,200 warships and more than 1,200 aeroplanes. A few hours earlier, more than 13,000 paratroopers descended on important defence points, such as bridges taken by the enemy (ONÇA, 2005, p.6-7). Among these soldiers, Martin was featured in the game.

After parachuting down alone on the outskirts of the small town of Ste. Mere-Eglise, Martin must neutralise a few German soldiers along the way until he finds his comrades. After surviving several battles in France, Martin is called up to take part in campaigns in Austria[45] , the Bavarian Alps in Germany and Belgium during the Battle of the Bulge .[46]

The official cover of the game, meanwhile, shows one of the front lines in France [Figure 8]:

Figura 8: Cover of Call of Duty (2003) for PC. Available at:

[45] In 1938, Austria was annexed to Germany by Hitler, forming a single state (CARDONA, 2009, p.20).

[46] A battle that took place between 16 and 26 December 1944 between the Germans and the Americans in the Ardennes Forest, Belgium. The country had been taken by the Nazis in 1940 (WILLMOT, 2008, p.234-235).

<http://2.bp.blogspot.com/_vUROHOKMYeQ/S7ih3qdd5oI/AAAAAAAAAA0/dPF4vRCDcFg/s1600/call+of+duty+1.jpg>, accessed 05 Mar. 2017.

Up until that point in the gaming universe, the presence of satisfactory artificial intelligence, in terms of the feeling of not being alone against your enemies, was still rather lacking[47] . Call of Duty relied on the artificial intelligence of companions, excluding the feeling of a "one-man army" exercised by the player. This characteristic can also be seen in Figure 8: the image suggests a photograph in which the protagonist is absent, but seems to be witnessing the scene. In it, the viewer is receiving an order from what appears to be his superior in the army hierarchy - probably Captain Foley, from whom the player must fulfil the orders given. Like the rest of his comrades in the image, the supposed leader is wielding a Garand M1[48] . His uniform characterises him as a member of the Airborne, due to the eagle crest on his left arm. On the side of his helmet, you can see the symbol of swords; like this one, the other symbols were distributed between squadrons of the same regiment to differentiate them - this one in Figure 8 was exclusive to the 506th *Parachute Infantry* Regiment (FALLSCHIRMJAGER, 2017), matching Martin's group.

As in *Medal of Honor Underground*, the setting is French because it is the only urban location available in the American campaign (the other missions with Martin take place in forests or tundras, for example). In addition to the ruined wall shown in the image, there are German soldiers firing anti-aircraft guns from a *Flakpanzer IV*[49] . The destruction of anti-aircraft guns is one of the objectives in a certain passage in the very first moments of the *game*, after the protagonist and his companions have neutralised the German enemies. In turn, it is Martin who must find a way to destroy them - the order that the viewer seems to receive in Image 8 is

[47] Some FPSs already had collaborative artificial intelligence in combat against common enemies, albeit in a very limited way. These included Medal of Honor Frontline (EA, 2002) and Half-Life (Valve, 1998).
[48] The US Army's standard rifle during the Second World War, with a calibre of 7.62 mm, had a capacity of eight rounds per magazine and could fire up to 30 rounds per minute. Although it was semi-automatic, excluding the use of a bolt, it emitted a sound when it ran out of ammunition, which could indicate the vulnerability of the combatant at the *front* (LÚDEKE, 2011, p.36).
[49] German anti-aircraft gun divided into four models: *Mobelwagen, Ostwind, Wilberwind* and *Kugelblitz.* In the image, the model is a *Mobelwagen.* It was designed in 1943 and produced in 1944, being used mainly in France (MILITARY FACTORY, 2017).

precisely that.

As a vehicle for representations, the *game* reproduces the most varied aspects, and this does not exclude the orders given to soldiers. The objectives required directly by a superior, placing the player as a mere man who must earn his prestige, was a novelty in war games.

However, the fact that the captain points at the protagonist/spectator has a connection with the game's title. Literally translated as "Call of Duty", the title is written to suggest the use of raw, impenetrable metal. As a soldier, the player has a duty to fight for his country; as this is an American game, the suggestion of putting the player in the role of a soldier about to fight in a scenario as hostile as the one on the cover is a great way of emphasising the courage of America's men.

The representations present in the image reveal a permeation of the memory of American combatants in France, even though this is a fictitious image that nevertheless simulates historical passages. The image as an advert for a game, set in World War II, reveals the importance that an ordinary man has in combat - giving the impression that, in a military hierarchy, he is exempt from his own social and/or racial problems. As Peter Burke explains,

> (...) Images are unreliable sources, distorting mirrors. However, they compensate for this disadvantage by offering substantial evidence on another level, in such a way that historians can turn a defect into a quality. (...) Images are treacherous because art has its own conventions, it follows a curve of internal development as well as reaction to the outside world (2004, p.37).

Therefore, the heroism conveyed not only by the game's cover, but in the game itself, is exaggerated, if not non-existent. Nothing is known about Martin's private life, or that of the other protagonists featured - let alone what happens to them after the end of the war. A huge proportion of those who returned from the war, on leaving the Armed Forces, returned to poverty and had to deal with unemployment; many young Americans couldn't resist and entered the criminal life. In addition, the country was racially segregated - which explains the absence of black soldiers[50] in the

[50] At the beginning of the war, African-American soldiers were sent on missions to provide unarmed support: transport, supplies, maintenance, etc., but with the significant increase in casualties among soldiers at the front, the support of black soldiers in combat became indispensable. The 761st Tank Battalion, made up exclusively

US battalions of Call of Duty (NATIONAL WW2 MUSEUM, 2017). Given that the cover of the game does not show the protagonist, placing the viewer as the main figure in the image, regardless of their social class or race, it is important to remember that "the art of representation is almost always less realistic than it seems and distorts social reality" (BURKE, 2004, p.37). Little is known about the lives of the protagonists of FPS games.

Captain Price, the Brit from the SAS

In Call of Duty, the campaign with the British army puts the player through the perspective of Sergeant Evans, also starting after the parachute assault on D-Day. The character is a member of the 6ª *Airborne* Division *and* must assist the team with the seizure of important strategic points on the Caen Canal, in northern France.

The character who stands out in this campaign is the commander, Captain Price. The Englishman, a graduate of the SAS[51] , is always present in the campaign's missions, including when Evans is deployed as an agent of the same special service - just like in *Call of Duty 2,* whose appearances occur chronologically earlier.

Like Manon, Captain Price is based on a real character: SAS agent John McAleese, who became known as a British hero in 1980, together with his mates, after saving 19 hostages from the hands of terrorists at the Iranian embassy in London[52] (HORSFALL, 2017). Price and McAleese resemble each other not only in their acts of courage, but also in their phenotypes: Price also has stern expressions, a long moustache and clear eyes [Figure 9]:

of black soldiers, was nicknamed the "Black Panthers" (NATIONAL WW2 MUSEUM, 2017).

[51] *Special Air Service*, British tactical special forces created in 1941. Its agents were originally assigned to sabotage German supplies on the lines of North Africa, even taking part in attempts to kidnap General Rommel. Today, the SAS takes part in anti-terrorist and hostage release operations around the world (ELITE UK FORCES, 2017; MOORHOUSE, 2009, p. 226-227).

[52] According to the video at <http://www.thesun.co.uk/sol/homepage/features/3780753/John- McAleese-the-man-who-made-the-SAS-famous.html>, accessed 07 Mar. 2017.

Figure 9: Captain Price in Call of Duty 2 (2005). Image available at: <http://smg.photobucket.com/user/Westy543/media/Call%20of%20Duty%202/cptpricecod2jpg.jpg.html>, accessed 07 Mar. 2017.

Price's role in the game is to guide the player (in the same way that Captain Foley gives orders in the American campaign). He seems to be immortal, because even if he is hit by machine-gun bursts or grenade explosions, he always survives, reacting as if every damage to his body was only a glancing blow. His immortality, like that of all the other important characters in the storyline, was designed so as not to present any inconsistencies, such as that of a vulnerable leader, the annoyance of constant game overs[53] and the strange task of an inferior in the military hierarchy having to pay attention to the success or failure of his commander. In electronic action games, it's common for the player to have to defend certain characters, usually unarmed or in need of an escort - but not with a highly trained officer. Unlike

Allied characters in Call of Duty who have no importance in the plot, i.e. they serve exclusively to add action and immersion to the battles, are mortal. When they die,

[53] Game over is the generic name given to a player's defeat in a game (losing a race, dying to an enemy, etc.). With the addition of checkpoints in games, the term has slowly been dropped in its literal sense, to be replaced by, for example, try again or restart, among others, according to the objectives of their respective producers. Classic Call of Duty games feature famous lines from strategists, military men and other historical figures, all related to war.

however, they are replaced by others, who soon join the battlefront.

In any case, Price is charismatic for several reasons: his physiognomy resembles that of a mentor, a father: although he has rigid features, he always knows what to do, even in moments of great tension. He treats his companions faithfully and doesn't hesitate to sacrifice himself for them. He also displays obvious traits of morality: in a particular mission in Call of Duty 2, two German soldiers are taken hostage in the backyard of a house. In the backyard, there are several wounded American soldiers who have been taken prisoner of war. In turn, these German guards promptly surrender when the British arrive. Price strongly orders these soldiers not to be executed - if the player doesn't comply, the game is over.

Moral traits like this apply to the "myth of the hero" more than to his physical characteristics. Although Price is a brave and offensive fighter, neutralising countless enemies in his path, he seems to seek to be fair in the face of unarmed foes. Such courtesies were not uncommon between combatants on opposing sides, depending on their commanders and the nation they were fighting for (given the massacres of civilians by both sides between the Germans and the Soviets, for example, this courtesy was in practice non-existent). Among several examples, we can cite the capture of two elite British soldiers, Roy Wooldridge and George Lane, by German soldiers. The prisoners were invited by General Erwin Rommel himself to join him for tea and sandwiches - a forbidden act among Third Reich officers. What's more, Rommel defied official protocol by putting them in an officers' prison instead of being shot. Both prisoners survived the war (CALZAVARA, 2014; SALKELD, 2014).

Although, modelled on the example above, Price didn't "offer tea and sandwiches" to his enemies, he firmed up his charisma with the cordiality of keeping them alive, unlike what happens reciprocally between Russians and Germans throughout the series (as will be seen later in the text). Although Germany was responsible for the deaths of thousands of British civilians between July and December 1940[54] , Price was able to distinguish between the various responsibilities of his

[54] Around 23,000 civilians were killed and 32,000 wounded during the German aerial bombardment of England - on 19 December alone, 3,000 people were killed. A relatively small number compared to the fatalities in France and Germany, for example (VÁZQUEZ, 2009, p.131).

enemies.

Price's heroism was the reason for his death on 27 October 1944 on board the German battleship Tirpitz[55] . Protecting Evans while he planted bombs on the ship in the company of another agent, Price was overwhelmed by the machine guns of several Germans. Although the captain also took part as commander in the second game, the mission on the Tirpitz in the first title was chronologically his last.

Stalinist fanaticism in the Red Army

Unlike the Americans and British featured in Call of Duty, Soviet soldiers, especially the commissars, are extremely aggressive, even towards their comrades. When playing the Soviet campaign of the first two games, the player can see numerous references to the fanaticism of some of these commissars towards Red Army soldiers who are hesitant to fight.

The Soviet campaign featured in the first Call of Duty is a clear reference to the feature film Circle of Fire[56] , in which the Russians cross the Volga to retake Red Square; despite the German gunfire, they still have to worry about the commissars' accusations of cowardice. Many passages in the film seem like déjà-vu to those who play Call of Duty.

The first mission of the Soviet campaign takes place at the crossing of the Volga River at Stalingrad[57] , on 18 September 1942. Several Soviet soldiers are transported on rafts, with commissars shouting into megaphones. On one of the transports is Alexei Ivanovich Voronin, the player-controlled protagonist of the campaign, a member of the 3rd Shock Army, 150ª Rifle Division. While the Germans speak in German, the Russians in the *game* speak in English - with a strong Slavic

[55] The battleship Tirpitz began to be built in 1936 alongside its twin model, the Bismarck (DE PAULA, 2014, p.110).

[56] "Circle of Fire" (2000), from the original Enemy at Gates, portrays the true story of sniper Vasily Zaitsev (Jude Law), considered the best sniper of the Second World War (YOSHIDA, 2008, p.38).

[57] The scene of the most violent battle fought between the Soviets and the Germans between August 1942 and February 1943. The city, destroyed by constant German bombing, became a pile of ruins and rubble. With a numerical advantage, as well as using the harsh winter cold and their knowledge of urban tactics to their advantage, the Soviets forced the Germans to surrender for the first time in the history of the *Third Reich*. Led by Marshal Georgi Zhukov, the Red Army then advanced eastwards until it reached Berlin in 1945 (GOMES, 2009, p.55 and JORGENSEN, 2007, p.215-221).

accent and a lot of "erres". This makes the game easier for Americans who, with or without the use of subtitles, are guided by their own language, as if the lines were dubbed.

The player and Alexei watch the commissioner who, with his robust voice, speaks fervently to his compatriots:

> Comrades, this day will be the proudest day you've ever lived! You will fight the fascist Nazi invaders with all your strength! For each and every fallen Soviet soldier, you will make them pay with ten of theirs. There will be no mercy for defeatists, cowards or traitors. Anyone caught deserting his post, will... be... shot! Remember, great Comrade Stalin's orders: Not one step backward. You will be well equipped for the battles that lie ahead. You will have food, water, weapons and plenty of ammunition. What did you suppose the Germans had? Nothing! Their supply lines are stretched too thin; their dash to the Volga has left them without the strength to bring us a proper fight. With our superior strength and numbers, and our boundless courage, victory is ours! We shall stop the Fascist invaders there - at Stalingrad![58]

During this monologue, German Ju-87 Stuka[59] planes attack the ferries twice. In the meantime, many frightened Soviet soldiers jump out of their boats in panic, but the commissars fire their guns at their own comrades, calling them cowards and traitors.

The commissar's optimism about the "unbalanced" Germans, however, only serves as an illusion to encourage his Soviet comrades; after all, they didn't have as many resources as the player might imagine. On returning to the west bank of the Volga with his companions, the player/protagonist is placed in a queue for the distribution of equipment. In turn, in the order of the queue, one receives a rifle and the next an ammunition cartridge. A commissioner announces that if the first one dies, the one carrying the ammunition is allowed to take the gun from his fallen comrade. Alexei

---

[58] "Comrades, this day will be the proudest day you have ever lived! You will fight the invading Nazifascists with all your might! For each and every fallen Soviet soldier, you will make them pay with ten of their own. There will be no mercy for deserters, cowards or traitors! Anyone caught disowning their post will... be... shot! Remember, orders from the great Comrade Stalin: no steps backwards. You will be well-equipped for the battles that lie ahead. You'll have food, water, weapons and a good amount of ammunition. What do the Germans have? Nothing! Their supply lines have been reduced to squalor; their crossing of the Volga has left them without the strength to fight us properly. With our superior strength and numbers, and our unlimited courage, victory is ours! We must stop the fascist invaders there - at Stalingrad!"

[59] A dive and close attack bomber with a top speed of 410 km/h and a flight range of 1,535 kilometres. It carried two 7.92 mm MG17 machine guns at the front and an MG81z machine gun at the rear. It could carry a maximum of 1800kg in bombs. An essential machine in the *Blitzkrieg*, it was highly effective against tanks and small groups of infantry (LÚDEKE, p.190-191, 2011).

doesn't get a gun, so he has to support his mate.

So throughout the first mission, the protagonist doesn't use a weapon. His companion, if the player is inattentive, easily disappears; but if he can keep up with him, he is destroyed by bombs and his weapon is not found in the confusion. And not only does the protagonist have to watch out for the endless German machine-gun fire, but he also has to make sure he doesn't go too far back in the scenario: otherwise he'll be machine-gunned by his mates as a traitor.

Further on, however, Alexei meets a Soviet sniper who asks him to help him eliminate one of the commissars, who is strategically preventing his comrades from retreating to find the communications equipment needed to call in artillery support. To do this, Alexei distracts the commissar and the sniper kills him.

Fanaticism and gratuitous murder were not uncommon, just as the game depicts. At the same time as Hitler was ordering the murder of millions in Germany, Stalin was doing the same in the Soviet Union, with his own people, accusing them all of conspiring against "Mother Russia". In many situations during the war, families in Russia didn't know which was worse: the USSR soldiers themselves, or the Germans. The author of the book "Stalin's Madness", Constantine Pleshakov, tells how his family fell victim to both the Communists and the Nazis:

> My grandmother, Anna Fedorovna Zimina (...) witnessed horrific scenes: during the civil war, the communists murdered her father in their backyard; a few years later, during the so-called "collectivisation" period implemented by Stalin, her family was evicted from their home and stripped of all their belongings; at the height of the Great Terror, she was accused of sabotage and almost lost her life. (...) When the Soviets began to evacuate the city, Anna and her husband were ordered to blow up the power station where they worked. But before they could fulfil this terrible task, the Red Army fled, leaving the plant and the family in the hands of the Germans. During the German occupation, (...) she [Anna] and her six-year-old daughter - who would later become my mother, Elza - were machine-gunned by Romanian soldiers (fortunately for me, (...) they were drunk and so they missed) (PLESHAKOV, 2008, p.18-19).

The Red Army itself, as already mentioned, was also a direct victim of the fanaticism of some military officers. In the next Call of Duty mission, a precise continuation of the previous one, the Soviets must reconquer Red Square.

At the beginning, some Soviet soldiers retreat and are presented as frightened by the bursts of gunfire from the German MG42[60] waiting for them on the other side of the square. However, they are killed by shots fired once again by the commissars themselves, who judge them as traitors and cowards. While advancing against the German enemies, Alexei finally acquires the gun of a dead comrade. The long mission ends with the taking of the square.

After several missions in which the player witnesses the Red Army's counter-attack from the Soviet Union to Germany, there is finally Call of Duty's 26ª mission, which presents the last day of combat between the two nations.
The mission takes place on the morning of 30 April 1945, during the siege of Berlin, near the Reichstag.

The Reichstag, the German parliament, was a symbol of the Third Reich and still fulfils its function in Germany today. On 28 April 1945, the Soviet army saw it for the first time. The following day, it was stopped on the banks of the River Spree by the German resistance. On the 30th, however, they crossed the river, but not without receiving several casualties *on Konigsplatz*, in front of the parliament - the resistance was practically made up of Nazi-fanatic Germans, fighting with all their might for Hitler's ideals and without any fear of death. The Soviets fought for hours until they managed to break through the siege and enter the gates of the Reichstag, whose interior was still defended by the last German soldiers (REGALADO, 2009, p.120).

In the game, the battle takes place up until the moment they take the parliament, but with a brief battle inside; most of the mission takes place outside. Together with other men from his group, Alexei reaches the top of the Reichstag and a fighter on the edge of it holds up the flag of the Soviet Union, informing the soldiers below that the building has been taken. However, this is not a precise allusion to the famous image photographed on that occasion by Yevgeni Khaldei (this subject will be duly returned to later in the text) .[61]

[60] Feared German support machine guns with a high rate of fire, it supported 7.92 mm ammunition and fired 1500 rounds per minute, with 50 or 250-round cartridges. The best machine gun of the Second World War (LÚDEKE, 2011, p.14).
[61] In Call of Duty: World at War (2009), the episode is repeated with another group of Soviets, even taking place in scenarios already seen in the first game in the series.

In real life, however, courageous figures like those portrayed in the game were never really heroicised during the communist dictatorship. Marshal Zhukov was one of those most responsible for the Nazi defeat until the siege of Berlin, and was beloved by Stalin himself, but not by his successor, Nikita Krushev:

> Zhukov became defence minister. But Krushev distrusted his loyalty and sent him into permanent retirement in 1957, even removing him from the defence ministry's party organisation. Until the end of his life, the marshal was reduced to a Party cell on the premises of a machinery factory, to his deep humiliation (PLESHAKOV, 2008, p.238).

While in the first Call of Duty the Soviets are portrayed as fanatical, merciless towards their own comrades, in the second game they appear as united, fighting together to complete their objectives - although ideologically they are equally in favour of the physical elimination of the Nazis, as can be seen in the first mission: a German prisoner is executed with a pistol shot (a very different attitude to that of Captain Price in the British campaign). Although the passages "denouncing" episodes present in the Soviets' campaign are a way of emphasising exacerbated patriotism, at the same time, blind fanaticism, courage and numerical superiority would be the only way to stop the enemy; after all, in strategy, the Soviets played a terrible role: since the Red Army's first campaigns in 1939, the Soviet Union's worst strategists were deployed to fight their enemies - this year, their forces turned to Finland, which resisted bravely throughout the war. The Soviets' strategic failure was mainly due to the Great Purge, from which Zhukov, probably the nation's most brilliant marshal, had escaped (LOSADA, 2009, p.18-19).

In this purge, Stalin, from 1937 onwards, began to imagine that a large number of his most important officers were plotting against him (many German spies even contributed to this paranoia by planting false documents accusing his officers). As a result, Stalin expelled 38,000 officers and commissars; men previously led by vozhd's rival Leon Trotsky were executed - three marshals, eleven commissar generals, all the district commanders, the chiefs of staff of the armed forces and hundreds of generals. They were mostly war veterans and great strategists. The elimination of these men left a gaping hole in the Soviet Union's strategic brilliance, so that its success against the Nazifascists was due to the numerical superiority of the Red Army's soldiers (LOSADA, 2009, p.11).

It's quite likely that Americans with patriotic feelings, when playing Call of Duty, will feel comfortable controlling the skin of a compatriot, or an Englishman, helping each other on the front against the Nazis during the Second World War. On the other hand, playing as a Soviet may seem unusual, as you realise the reality of a nation that, ideologically, is so far away.

Representations of Germans at the front

In the Call of Duty series, German enemies were innovated in a way that had never been seen before in games. They were no longer represented by using harsh features on their faces or bodies. Deep-set eyes and severely angled faces, as in Medal of Honor and Wolfenstein 3D, were no longer features.

Already in the first Call of Duty, it is noticeable that many of the Germans have faces that correspond to Western ideals of masculine beauty, well-adorned, no longer just cruel or severe. But these representations do not exclude the presence of others who appear in contrary conditions. Among the enemies, for example, obese men have now been presented (ironically, no allies have been depicted in this way). Some even keep their moustaches in the same shape as Hitler's, denouncing the ideological fervour of many soldiers at the front.

These innovations were probably designed to make it clear to the player that this is a war game, and like any war, armies are generally made up of ordinary people, among whom the number of those who fight purely out of duty is quite high, while others fight for ideological reasons. In Nazi Germany, there are many testimonies of military dissatisfaction with Hitler's policies, not excluding those who had once been fanatical about National Socialism but ended up being disappointed by the increasingly authoritarian policies - in addition to the growing general knowledge of the concentration camps. For example, Admiral Wilhelm Canaris, head of espionage for the Abwehr[62] , manipulated communications in order to benefit the British to the detriment of the expansion of the Reich; or the so-called Operation Walkiria, in which Wehrmacht Colonel Claus von Stauffenberg, together with high-ranking German officers, organised and carried out a bomb attack on Hitler in 1944; among the plotting officers were Erwin Rommel and Wilhelm Canaris (BASSETT, 2005, pp.129-153; MOORHOUSE, 2009, p.247-301).

The question of fighting for Germany and not for Nazism was emphasised by many German war veterans after the fall of the Third Reich. Psychiatrist Leon Goldensohn interviewed Karl Donitz, the admiral and Hitler's successor who was responsible for Germany's surrender to the Allies. Recalling that the German was on trial pending in Nuremberg after the war[63] , Goldensohn wrote:

> I asked him what he thought of the "Führer principle[64] ". He replied that he had never been in favour of it, because a man always needs a "corrective". That's why a head of state needs a chief of state and other counsellors. Would he have opposed Hitler in any way, by any actions or expressive opinions? No. He was a man of the sea, and that was all. Most of the atrocities, he believes, were committed by Austrians, or at least the Bavarians (...): "I realise how impossible this [the extermination programmes] must sound to an American. It's something that couldn't happen in a democracy. But in our kind of government, it was possible" (GOLDENSOHN, 2005, p.39-40).

On both sides of the conflict, it was common for soldiers to disown or surrender in the face of enemies with a numerical advantage. In this new version, the game has probably made an effort to engage in dialogue from these perspectives.

In keeping with this trend, another novelty in Call of Duty is the emotional aspect of the soldiers. Again following the example of the German soldiers surrendered by Captain Price's soldiers, one of them pleads: "Don't shoot, please!
Nicht schiefien! We have wounded here!" [65] - which again shows that these are ordinary

---

[62] Intelligence service of the Third Reich, responsible for espionage and counterespionage (BASSETT, 2007, p.101).
[63] The trial held by Allied authorities from 1945 onwards convicted more than 20 leading Nazi figures (GELLATELY, 2005, p.7).
[64] Capitalised here because of the reference to Hitler, not the title fuhrer, the head of state.
[65] The English subtitles read, "Don't shoot, please! Please listen to me! We have wounded here!"; however, the

people sent to war. If the two soldiers were depicted as Nazi fanatics, the wounded prisoners would probably be dead or under torture (even under the emphatic order of a superior in the military hierarchy, the soldiers could disobey it due to the close fighting). This would serve as a pretext for murdering the prisoners without them taking the blame). You also realise that the surrendered enemy seems to get lost in his English speech, mixing it with German. Unlike the first Medal of Honor, the enemy now speaks their original language in Call of Duty. During battles, the command shouts remain in the original German, recorded by German voice actors - the pronunciation is correct and doesn't hint at any foreign accent, emphasising the immersion of the combat atmosphere.

On the other hand, characteristics that "humanise" the Germans in the course of the games do not make them omissive subjects; on the contrary, they are represented as well-trained and aggressive soldiers in the face of the Allied advance. As in the aforementioned Soviet campaign, they fight with intense aggression to defend parliament at the end of the first game; in Call of Duty 2, one of the most difficult passages in the game occurs during the American campaign, in which the protagonist, who landed in the Omaha sector during D-Day, must retreat from a portion already held by the Allies to return to the coastal portion. On the way to the starting point, the waves of enemy soldiers are literally infinite: if the player doesn't advance little by little through the scenario, the respawn[66] of German combatants occurs over and over again.

Although Call of Duty presents different perspectives on the battles, there is no campaign to play as an Axis soldier. The reasons are obvious: the production company is American, and playing as a German fighter, for example, would be an allusion to the defence of Nazism. On the other hand, in the *online* multiplayer mode - from the first title to the most recent one on the subject, *World at War* - you can fight as a German soldier. The difference between this option *and Battlefield 1942* is the uncensored display of Nazi ideology, which means that military flags and coats of arms emblazoned with swastikas have not been omitted (although in its competitor, *Medal*

translation from German to English is erroneous, as "nicht schiePen" means "don't shoot".

[66] A term used in the gamer world to refer to the reappearance of the same figure, replacing one that has already been eliminated.

of Honor, these allusions have been removed).

In any case, the *Call of Duty* titles have managed to convey both the brutality of the German army and the presence of seemingly ideologically detached soldiers among the combatants, while the Allies are similarly portrayed in terms of their respective concepts of idealism or political indifference.

The almost unnoticed reference to the Poles

The third game in the series, *Call of Duty 3*, from 2006, still maintains the missions in which you can play as a soldier from the British and American armies, excluding the campaigns on the eastern *front* to give exclusivity to the west. Compared to the previous games in the franchise, the third title was quite repetitive as it had an almost linear plot sequence. It was released exclusively for the consoles .[67]

The game's novelty lay in the variety of nations the player fought for: as well as British and American soldiers, you could play as a Canadian, a Frenchman and a Pole. Playing as a Canadian or a Pole was a novelty in the world of games depicting war (Manon had already permeated the importance of French combatants).

In *Call of Duty 3*, there are only two missions concerning the Polish fighter: the seventh and thirteenth. In them, the player controls Private Bohater Woychek of the Polish 1ª Armoured Division. The first of these missions is a pursuit by him and his comrades of the German tank commander Richter, nicknamed Black Baron, one of those responsible for the German campaign against Poland. The pursuit takes place using a tank Sherman Firefly[68] , which the player controls. Throughout the mission, the player must destroy Panzer tanks and infantry units. In the end, you must destroy the Panzer II operated by Officer Richter, who is never physically shown. The other mission with the Pole, this one on foot, also takes place in Nazi-occupied France.

On the other hand, the game's reference to the Polish soldier and his comrades is not much of an homage, starting with the setting: it's not set in Poland, but

[67] *Playstation 2*, *Playstation 3*, *Xbox*, *Xbox 360* and *Wii*.

[68] British version of the American *Sherman M4* tank. It could reach 46 km/h and had a 7.6 cm cannon and 7.62mm M1919 A4 machine guns (LÚDEKE, 2011, p.132-133).

in France. In its context, the Polish characters are survivors of the Nazi-Soviet massacre[69] and continued to fight alongside their allies on the Western front. It's true that a large part of Poland's military contingent was transferred to fight outside the country, but that doesn't mean that the Poles didn't fight bloody battles on their own territory. Quite the opposite: resistance to the German and Soviet advance worried both Hitler and Stalin's top brass. Despite being outnumbered and outgunned - and the frustrating failure of the Allies to fulfil their promise to help fight the invasion - the Poles held out on both *fronts* for 36 days[70] (CARDONA, 2009, p.7-29).

Call of Duty 3 doesn't seem to want to show the battles that were lost by the Allies. Although the Polish resistance was strong, fuelled by intense hatred of the invading communists and fascists, it was inferior in terms of military contingent and arsenal. On the *gaming* scene, the lack of reference to the countries involved in the war is still gigantic, with the exception of the US, British and Soviet nations that have been referenced several times (the latter alongside Germany, in terms of the number of games that portray them as enemies). The triplet of nations favoured for involvement in the fighting only seems more interesting, on the part of the producers, because they fought in greater numbers against the Axis - and won. The player who knows which countries were involved in the defeat of Germany, Italy and Japan, for example, has the feeling that if they play an Alliance protagonist, they are on their way to inevitable victory (each campaign mission being chronologically more decisive than the last). Nations like Brazil, Finland and anti-fascist Italy, among others, were also victorious, but with a relatively smaller military contingent - which doesn't mean that the battles they were involved in were any less intense.

In any case, although the first three canonical Call of Duty games were responsible for conveying various representations of the Second World War, the fifth

[69] Hitler ordered the invasion of the country on 1 September from the west, and Stalin on 17 September from the east, in partnership (CARDONA, 2009, p.13-14), as a result of the non-aggression pact signed between Ribbentrop and Molotov in 1939. Poland was the first country to be invaded with active resistance, without receiving help, as promised, from the British and French allies. Both the Germans and the Soviets were responsible for the mass murder of Polish civilians (VÁZQUEZ, 2009, p. 127-137).

[70] In particular, the German attack lasted from 1 to 15 September 1939, and the Soviet attack from 17 September to 6 October of the same year (CARDONA, 2009, p.7-29).

game in the series presented an extremely violent and brutal aspect, never before seen in games about this historical event.

Call of Duty: World at War (2008)

After a "truce" with the theme of "World War II" - since *Call of Duty 4 - Modern Warfare* (2007) was set in a contemporary context - the production company *Treyarch* released, at least until now, the last *Call of Duty* game depicting the Second World War, under the title *World at War* (2008). The game was released for PC, *Playstation 3*, *Xbox 360* and *Wii* (as well as extremely reduced versions for *Playstation 2* and *Nintendo DS*). The cover is as shown in Figure 10.

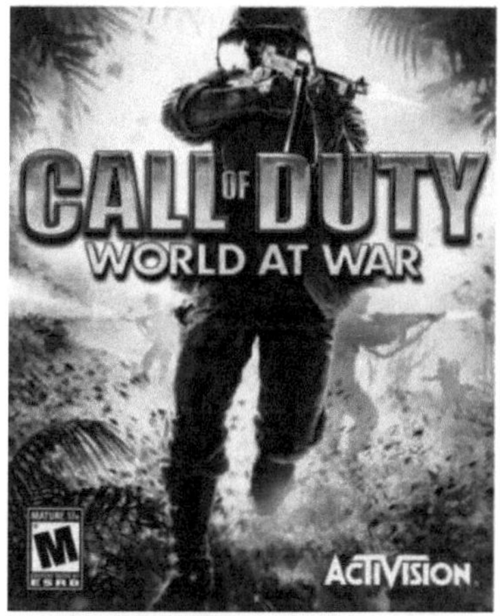

Figure 10: North American cover of Call of Duty: World at War (2008). Available at:< http://3.bp.blogspot.com/-YddlI4PmemA/TpR1iewzymI/AAAAAAAAAE0/FmA_j4bvu5Y/s1600/call-of-duty-world-at-war-400x5681.jpg>, accessed 13 Mar. 2017.

Unlike the previous games, this title was divided into two campaigns, featuring two characters on different fronts: Private C. Miller, from the United States, and Private Dimitri Petrenko, from the Soviet Union. The perspectives of the two are disparate and present very contrasting contexts, as we'll see below.

It's important to emphasise that in the production credits there is no mention of the consultants who helped shape the game's storyline, but rather a thank you to the veterans, named one by one, who shared their stories and memories; in turn, these thank yous are addressed solely to the members of the First Marine Division Veterans

Association, all Americans. Although we can't expect every player to read these messages, it's clear that they're a form of reverence for the combatants who fought in the Second World War. However, it is not a question of paying homage to all the combatants, but only to those who fought in the name of the right cause: that of the Allies. It can be concluded that, in the absence of specific advisors, the game's plot was created from the compilation of stories told by veterans to the team.

The wave of freedom sweeps the Japanese empire

When the player of Call of Duty: World at War selects the "new game" option, they are shown animated infographics that inform them about the context of the war between the Japanese and the Americans, without any narration. Real videos, which refer to situations presented as "Japanese atrocities" committed against the Chinese during the so-called Sino-Japanese War[71] , are shown.

The massacre of the Chinese moved various authorities around the world, including the United States, which, as punishment - as shown in the game's infographic - signed a 90 per cent embargo on oil exports to the Japanese. In response to this humiliating embargo, Emperor Michinomiya Hirohito ordered the air attack on the American base of Pearl Harbor, which took place on 7 December 1941, triggering the declaration of war by the United States against the Axis (JURADO, 2009, p.87-93).

After presenting the infographic, the game puts the player in the perspective of Miller, who is inside a wooden hut on Makin atoll[72] , on 17 August 1942. He has his hands tied behind his back along with his mate, K. Pyle; both are members of the 1st [a] *Marine* Division, 2nd Battalion of the *Marine Raiders.*

A Japanese officer, who is shown smoking a cigar, interrogates them both,

[71] With the rise of Bolshevism in Russia, Japan supported the Tsarist government, but with the defeat of the Mensheviks, they withdrew from the neighbourhood of the Siberian Lake Baikal in 1922. However, in 1931, China found itself weakened by diplomatic tensions: the new leader of the Kuomitang (Chinese Nationalist Party), Chiang Kai-Chek, had broken his alliance with the Soviet Socialists. Japan quickly sent its troops back to Manchuria, creating a satellite state on Chinese territory - which led the League of Nations, in 1933, to condemn the Japanese brutality towards Chinese civilians (DE PAULA, 2015, p. 103-104).

[72] Island under British mandate in the *Gilbert Islands* archipelago in the Central Pacific, taken by the Japanese in 1941 (GALEANO, 2009, p.96).

while his soldier beats Pyle with a bamboo [Figure 11]. Pyle spits in the officer's face, who wipes himself with the sleeve of his uniform and responds by poking the prisoner in the eye with the lit cigar. He then orders his subordinate to execute him - he draws his *katana and* cuts Pyle's neck. He then turns to Miller, but before he can execute him in the same way, he is silently murdered by *sailors* Roebuck and Sullivan.

Figure 11: Private Pyle is hit with a bamboo moments before being executed. Available at:< http://vignette2.wikia.nocookie.net/callofduty/images/e/ef/World_at_War_Pyle_being_tortured.jpg/revision/latest?cb=20120329175252>, accessed 13 Mar. 2017.

While inside the hut, the player can't move Miller, leaving him with the option of watching the scene. The character can be controlled from the liberation of his companions, and outside the hut, the player comes across several dead American soldiers tied to wooden logs (in Figure 11, on the right-hand side, you can see two soldiers who probably correspond to Roebuck and Sullivan. During the game, this perspective is not possible, as the Japanese officer is in front of the player's view. Figure 11 was probably edited to centre the torture of the American).

After battles between the Americans and the Japanese, the scenery suddenly becomes quiet as the player and his team make their way through a dark forest. They come across a temple lit by torches. One of the men approaches to investigate, at which point he is caught in a trap and instantly blown up by Japanese bombs. Pieces of his body scatter to the sides, along with a torrent of blood dripping from his mutilated carcass. Soon afterwards, a unison "Banzai[73] " is heard, shouted by Japanese soldiers who suddenly emerge from the bush and advance on the Americans with the bayonets of their rifles.

Never before in Call of Duty have the deaths been so violent, with the trap against the American serving as a prelude to the content that follows. The series title's[74] engine now allowed for more realistic combat, without any censorship of violence.

These passages from the first mission belittle the Japanese soldiers: they are depicted as savages, they carry out cruel ambushes and traps, and they fight without caring about their lives, always in the name of the emperor. This idea is further emphasised at the beginning of the mission, inside the hut: the Japanese don't hesitate to get blood on themselves, nor do they show any mercy to the enemy.

Representing the enemy in this way is a "clear form of propaganda that offers the opportunity to portray the commander in a heroic light" (BURKE, 2004, p.184), so that the American in the game, while a victim of Japanese violence, is at the same time a liberator of the Pacific.

The representation of the Other in the game is emphatic when it comes to the "horrors of war": possibly the transfer of the memory of war veterans consulted for the creation of the game, in this sense, was quite emphatic. Such a transfer, however, is an old habit: since the 15th century, soldiers were sent to the front to record the events of the fighting and permeate them through the visual arts (BURKE, 2004, p.185). This doesn't mean, however, that the battles in the Pacific weren't violent, but the game only highlights the psychological terrorism, in terms of violence, of the Japanese on the Americans - and never the other way round.

The continuation of the American character's campaign in World at War takes place approximately two years later, on 15 September 1944. Now, Miller takes part in a landing on White Beach in Peleliu[75] . As soon as the mission begins, with the

[73] Also said in its original form, tenno heika banzai, it means "long live the Emperor".

[74] A package of functions present in a game that allows several interactions in it at the same time. It is responsible for the texture, sounds, artificial intelligence and physical interaction of a game. Currently, the same engine can integrate different games - it is chosen by the producer (KLEINA, 2011).

[75] An island in the Palau archipelago about 10 kilometres long and 500 metres wide at its centre. On the day

countless rafts crossing the sea, the player feels overwhelmed by the grandeur of the Allied ships in the background and the number of comrades about to disembark. A cliché moment in games that simulate landings[76] occurs when the raft reaches the sand: it is blown up by an enemy bomb and the protagonist sinks, with a view similar to that of the feature film Saving Private Ryan[77] ; the player sees what is underwater, with bullets passing through the water and leaving trails of bubbles. When the protagonist emerges, he calls for naval support via radio, eliminating the accumulation of enemies protecting the edge of the beach.

Soon afterwards, another impressive passage is presented in the game: burning Japanese soldiers stagger inertly towards the Americans like the undead. At this point, the player can shoot them, putting an end to their agony. If the player does nothing, the enemies simply drop dead. The visual impact of the soldiers' suffering, even if they are enemies, probably tends to make the player feel moved to understand them as mere men, incapable of any evil; they don't scream, as if redeeming themselves for their war crimes, making the scene more cruel. Whereas previously the Japanese enemy was belittled, now it reappears in the form of impotent combatants, incapable of redeeming themselves.
defend and attack. They are no longer emphatic fighters in their ideology, but simple creatures who, now harmless, are a reference to the destructive power of man. In flames, they don't have their features; they are represented as ordinary men, but blinded and killed for the cause they were fighting for. If these soldiers are looking for redemption after death, however, it is quite ironic that they stagger towards the American platoons.

In the game's chronology, the third mission is a direct continuation of the battle of Peleliu. As the game loads this mission, an infographic displays a coffin where Sergeant Sullivan, killed in the previous mission, lies. This coffin quickly turns into a

---

of the landing, 12 September, it was supported by amphibious assault guns with 37 mm and 75 mm cannons. The Japanese guarded the Palau Islands with 21,000 soldiers from the imperial army, 7,000 from the navy and 10,000 labourers. On Peleliu alone, there were 13,500 men (GALEANO, 2009, p.37-63).

[76] Scenes like this had already been shown in Medal of Honor: Frontline and Call of Duty 2, for example.

[77] Saving Private Ryan (1998), directed by Steven Spielberg, tells the story of Captain Miller (Tom Hanks) and his group of Marines who land on D-Day with the mission of rescuing a soldier (RIBEIRO, 2008, p.19).

star inside the United States flag - a visible tribute to the thousands of American soldiers who died fighting for their country over seventy-five years ago.

After missions from the Soviet campaign, as will be shown later, the game resumes missions from the Pacific front. Miller carries a flamethrower, and according to Sergeant Roebuck, "We need to get our hands dirty. Flamethrowers. We'll burn them. This line indirectly suggests that the Americans had not "got their hands dirty" up to this point (alluding to the fact that shooting and bombing were part of a "fair game" against the Japanese). They considered themselves immaculate until the need to use fire as a weapon.

From now on, the missions still take place in Peleliu. This one, in particular, takes place inside trenches, a place where the use of[78] flamethrowers was very common. In this mission, the weapon is used intensely, making it common to see enemy soldiers burning to death - some faster, others not so much. And because it takes place in a closed environment, the M1897 Trench Gun[79] also becomes indispensable. This high-impact weapon easily shatters the enemy in the same way as explosives and other high-calibre weapons.

Once again, you can see the producer's non-censorship of the war, represented with a very intense realism, for example in the display of wounded, mutilated and dead bodies. The bloodied bodies, if not burnt, are clearly mutilated: many are missing arms, legs or even their heads. As well as mutilating the enemy, the shot destroys a part of their body in such a way that you can see one of their lungs under the ribcage, for example. In many cases, even after losing an arm or a leg, the soldier is still in agony, crawling in his own pool of blood.

After the battles on Peleliu, Miller is sent to the island of Okinawa[80] with Sergeant Roebuck and Private Polonsky in 1945. During the loading of the mission,

---

[78] The flamethrower in World at War is an M-2 model, produced from 1944. It used nitrogen as a propellant (LÚDEKE, 2011, p.39).

[79] Shotgun, or rifle, created in 1897 by Winchester. It is a 12-gauge shotgun with a capacity of five + one projectiles (GUNS.COM, 2017).

[80] In Japanese territory, the island of Okinawa is 106 kilometres long and an average of 11 kilometres wide. With its volcanic soil, the island was of great importance to the Japanese as it served as a natural barrier to the East China Sea, where they established communication between Japan and the south-west Pacific, as well as a large number of aerodromes and military installations (GALEANO, 2009, p.119-125).

the sergeant states that the morale of the soldiers is low, so that the infographic indicates that the chances of survival are only one in five. Fatigue is visible through the representation of physical tiredness, low morale, a desire for revenge, among others. Roebuck speaks for the squad as a whole:

> Everything that was asked of us, we've done. Every night we lay in a filthy foxhole praying the enemy won't slit our throats. Every day we spent crawling through the mud and dirt while bullets whistled all around. But this is the last time we're going to have to put our lives on the line. This is the enemy's last stand. When we take Shuri Castle, we go home. All of us.[81]

The sergeant also receives information that Mount Shuri, historically one of the last Japanese lines of defence on Okinawa (GALEANO, 2009, p.130-131), the area they are to occupy, is practically deserted. However, the squadron finds itself without ammunition and must obtain it via a crate that has been sent by parachute. Once the supplies have been obtained, a wave of Japanese soldiers attacks the group with infantry and mortars.

Making their way up the hill, the squadron manages to penetrate Shuri Castle[82] , and by the end of the mission, they have to contain the hundreds of enemies well positioned in every room and part of the castle courtyards.

In the largest courtyard, three Japanese soldiers surrender. Roebuck orders his men to cease fire, and together with Polonsky, they search the surrendered men. Suddenly, the unarmed soldiers start pushing them back and two of them manage to remove the grenade pins, holding on to the Americans. The player must decide, in a short space of time, which of the two companions to save. By killing the enemy selected, the companion manages to dodge the explosion, but there's no time to save the second ally. Whichever choice is made, the surviving comrade revolts and hurls

---

[81] "Everything we were asked to do, we did. Every night we lie in a filthy trench praying that the enemy doesn't cut our throats. Every day we crawl through mud and dust while bullets whistle all around. But this is the last time we need to put our lives at risk. This is the enemy's last stand. When we take Castle Shuri, we're going home. All of us."

[82] A castle built in the 12th century and now a heritage site in the city of Naha, it served as the residence of King Sho Hashi. Covering 60,000 metres^2, the castle was partially destroyed during the Second World War (GALEANO, 2009, p.119; JAPAN ATLAS, 2017).

insults at the Japanese, who are now surging across the courtyard in gigantic waves. With air support, however, the battle for Shuri Castle is won.

The battle for Okinawa took place after Iwo Jima[83] , and the island was finally considered safe on 21 June 1945 (GALEANO, 2009, p.134). From then on, the United States could consider itself victorious over Japan, but the Second World War only officially ended on 2 September 1945, after attacks on Japanese civilians through the use of atomic weapons .[84]

The feeling that the game tries to convey, based on the intention of its producers, when you finish the missions with the Americans, is that they have fought against a cowardly enemy, especially when the soldiers surrender, but intend to kill themselves with their enemies. As if that wasn't enough, it gives the player the feeling that the Americans are liberators of the Pacific, where the Japanese Empire had taken possession of several islands. This ideal of liberating empires is a symbol of pride for those who call themselves democratic and try to present themselves that way.

At the same time, however, *World at War* conveys another kind of freedom against the Axis; on the Euro-Eastern *front*, it is not for democratic ideals that the enemy is being fought, but for a nation as totalitarian as Nazi Germany: the Soviet Union, once again depicted as fighting the Germans. This time, however, the purpose of the combatants is fuelled by an intense sense of hatred and revenge.

The ruthless Soviets: from Stalingrad to Berlin

At the end of the third mission of the US campaign, an infographic centres on a grey globe in Europe, with a swastika in place of Germany, and the red of the Nazi flag dominating the other regions of Europe (the two *fronts* presented in the game take turns in the order of the missions). This wave of colour reaches as far as Stalingrad. While showing images of the devastation of war, a hoarse voice[85] says the following

[83] An island of volcanic soil surrounded in 1944 by American submarines and only taken in February of the following year, after intense bombing and landings (LOSADA, 2009, p.18).
[84] The Fat Man and Little Boy atomic bombs devastated the Japanese cities of Nagasaki and Hiroshima respectively. Dropped by B-29 bombers, the attack resulted in more than 200,000 deaths and injuries. The photographer of the explosion, Bob Caron, vented his frustration at the moment the bomb devastated Hiroshima: "Goddamn, what a son of a bitch!" (NARLOCH, 2005, p.29-35).
[85] The voice is that of English actor Gary Oldman, who voiced Viktor Reznov in *Call of Duty: World at War*, according to the game's end credits.

words in English, with a strong Russian accent:

> The rotten cancer of the fascist *Reich* ravages Europe like a plague. Their relentless drive into our motherland steals the lives of men, women, and children alike. The arrogance of their leaders is matched only by the brutality of their soldiers. These are the darkest days of Nazi occupation of Stalingrad.[86]

The Russian part of the campaign begins in the middle of Red Square. The setting at the start of this mission could be nostalgic for the first *Call of Duty*, but the atmosphere and occasion presented are quite different.

With blurred vision, the controlled character wakes up inside the fountain in the square. Instead of water, the fountain is filled with the bodies of Soviet soldiers. A crow lands in front of him, but then takes off as a Panzer comes too close. German soldiers walk ahead, while others stand on the tank. They check the bodies closely and machine-gun those that move with their MP40s. The scene is reproduced in Figure 12:

Figure 12: Germans execute surviving Soviet soldiers. Available at: <http://www.mobygames.com/images/shots/l/405407-call-of-duty-world-at-war-xbox-360-screenshot-a-german-soldier.jpg>, accessed 13 Mar. 2017.

[86] "The rotten cancer of the fascist *Reich* is ravaging Europe like a plague. Its relentlessness enters the motherland stealing the lives of men, women and children alike. The arrogance of its leaders is ruled only by the brutality of its soldiers. These are the dark days of the Nazi occupation of Stalingrad".

The view remains static until the enemy moves away, while the protagonist plays dead. Then the name of the mission appears on the screen: Vendetta, the Italian word for "revenge". The screen also displays other information: the date, 17 September 1942[87] , and the name of the character being controlled: Dimitri Petrenko, of the 62ª Rifle Division .[88]

From then on, the player can move Petrenko around. The scenery is grey, destroyed by bombs; puddles of water mix with the blood of dead Russian soldiers, and there are flies, fire, smoke and several German bombers flying high overhead. Among the pile of bodies, a figure moves, having also played dead.

It's Sergeant Viktor Reznov, a defining character in the franchise. He is the embodiment of the Russian man's hurt, revenge, resentment and hatred of the German. After asking for silence with a brief "shhhh", his first line (translated) is: "do as I say, and we can avenge this massacre". It's the same voice of the man who narrates the mission infographic, while loading.

Reznov is hunting Heinrich Amsel, the general responsible for the massacre of Russian soldiers and civilians in the region. Dimitri sees the officer with some soldiers through the scope of a rifle, but Reznov explains to him that he has to be patient and that his hunt is like that of "any other animal".

The personification of Reznov as the aggrieved Soviet seeking revenge on the Nazi is a representation of the feeling of a nation devastated by the enemy. This emotion has become common throughout Europe. Unlike the United States, whose geographical location was not bombed, the Soviet Union was devastated by German bombs and thousands of civilians were killed. In the first twenty days of the German occupation of Soviet territory alone, Russia lost 600,000 of its three million combatants (PLESHAKOV, 2008, p.20).

The rivalry between Germany and the Soviet Union was ideological and

---

[87] The campaign with Alexei in the first Call of Duty takes place the next day.

[88] Later, he joins the 3rd Shock Army, 150th Rifle Division, just like Alexei in the first game.

intensified during the war, sometimes between communists and sometimes between National Socialists, so that physical elimination was an attribute always emphasised by the military leaders. Hitler hated communism and Stalin hated National Socialism. But, as in war, used in extreme measures, they became similar in their elimination of each other. Historian Joachim Fest, a reference in Hitler biographies, argues that the Nazi dictator's policy differed from Stalin's only in that it did not propose the insertion of a civilisational notion of peace for the future. On the contrary, it was governed by "greed and ambition, the two almost omnipresent motivating impulses in the endeavour to subjugate other peoples" (FEST, 2005, p.171).

And not just hurt, Sergeant Reznov is presented as a nostalgic chap. When he enters a pub, which he partially burns down, he says that the place "once echoed with conversations between friends and lovers. No more". He then re-emphasises his vengeful spirit: "Mark my words, comrade. One day, things will change. We will take our fight to your lands; your people; your blood." In this respect, the game's creators probably tried to convey the feelings of revenge and nostalgia that took hold among those who were victimised by the war that took place within their borders, as opposed to the notion of war formulated in distant America.

A few moments later, still on the same mission, Dimitri witnesses Reznov being ambushed by German soldiers. This depicts the use of psychological torture by the Germans against their enemies: while two of them surrender the sergeant with submachine guns, a third approaches carrying a flamethrower and fires it wildly upwards in order to show off his terrible weapon. Before he can burn Reznov alive, however, the Germans are targeted by a group of Soviets.

At the end of this mission, Dimitri kills the fugitive General Amsel with a sniper rifle shot. And just like the game's North American campaign, years pass after the first mission.

After the previous instalment of the game, three years pass, bringing us to 1945. Like the first mission with the Americans, Vendetta also served as a prelude to the last battles of the Second World War.

The game's infographic now states that Russian soldiers outnumbered the Germans ten to one, which historically means 220,000 men and 500 German tanks against 880,000 men, 3,000 tanks and 15,000 Soviet cannons (COSTILLA, 2009, p.100-101) - confirming the idea that the Soviets relied on numerical superiority to compensate for strategic failures.

The mission is now in Seelow. Matías Costilla explains the importance of the region in his infographic:

> The Seelow Hills formed the last line before reaching Berlin. The Soviet army was determined to take this natural barrier to the east of Berlin and finally managed to break through it, but at an exorbitant cost, both in men and material. (...) The disproportion of forces was extraordinary, but even so, it took the Soviets a long time to manage to open a breach. Zhukov planned to massacre the defences in a few hours and launch his attacks towards Berlin on the morning of 16 April (COSTILLA, 2009, p.100-101).

The game is set on 18 April, the day on which a German counter-attack supported by the Luftwaffe destroys several Soviet divisions (COSTILLA, 2009, p.100). The mission begins in a dark room in a farmhouse. Dimitri is on the floor and three Germans occupy the room without realising that he is alive. When he tries to pick up his dead mate's gun next to him, one of the Germans catches him and strikes him in the face, followed by a punch. Before he can do anything else, however, a T-34 tank[89] destroys part of the house and the Germans are hit. Reznov enters the place with another soldier, Chernov. The latter is ordered by the sergeant to "finish off those rats" - the Germans hit by the tank - but Chernov replies: "There's no point, sergeant... they're already bleeding to death!". Reznov finally says: "then maybe our friend will help them bleed out faster," while arming his mate Dimitri.

At this point, Reznov's promised revenge is already underway and lasts until the end of the game, favouring atrocities against Germans, including the surrendered. For his part, Chernov seems to be more rational and counterbalances the sergeant's fanaticism, often playing the role of good conscience against Reznov's ego. It is then up to the player to decide whether, as Chernov says, to let them bleed to death, but with

[89] Russian battle tank. It travelled at up to 50 km/h, had a range of 300 km and was armed with a 76 mm or 85 mm cannon and two 7.62 mm submachine guns (WILLMOTT, 2008, p.190).

still some chance of survival, or; to confirm their death by executing them as Reznov suggests. Moments that push the player to exercise their understanding of morality and ethics are common throughout the game, even more so during the Soviet campaign.

Reznov reaffirms his vengeful thirst: "now it's your land; your people; your blood," as he once promised at Stalingrad.

At the end of the mission, thanks to the violence applied by Dimitri in the fight against the Germans, Reznov gives him the chance to rest on a tank until a certain point in the mission. As for Chernov, he makes it clear: "Not you". Reznov considers Dimitri the true hero of Stalingrad; the merit of the rest comes from his use of violence, unlike Chernov.

Chronologically, the missions with the Soviet siege of Berlin take place before the last three of the American campaign. At the very beginning of the mission in which the Soviets reach Pankow, German soldiers surrender. Chernov again shows mercy:

- Sargent! There are survivors!

- These animals raped and marauded their way through the motherland without mercy!" [90]

One of the German soldiers shouts "nein, bitte!"[91] , but they are all machine-gunned.

One of the survivors, who lies dying on the ground, is then shot in the head with a pistol.

At the end of the same mission, a commissar uses a megaphone while several Russian tanks enter the capital. In the Portuguese translation, the commissioner shouts: "Citizens of Berlin! An iron ring surrounds your rotten city. We will crush all those who dare to resist the wrath of the Red Army".

The commissioners' warning to civilians is not a fictitious allusion. Joachim Fest recounts how a weakened resistance was put up in the German city:

[90] Translation of the two sentences in Portuguese: "Sergeant! There are survivors!" / "These animals have raped and murdered all over the motherland without mercy!".

[91] From the German "no, please!".

> Day after day, his [*Reich]* "Recruiting Squad" went out with the mission of scouring private companies and public services for civilians fit for the *front.* The numbers he presented, however, were no longer surprising, even after he had transformed that afflicted little group of civilians into a regiment impatient to go into action in the fight for the *Fuhrer* and the Fatherland. (...) Each civilian who was part of the combat troop had, and only if he had a rifle, ammunition for five shots (FEST, 2005, p.37).

Civilians therefore found themselves in a delicate situation. On the one hand, the Soviets threatened them if they helped the Nazis; on the other, the Nazis threatened them if they co-operated with the Soviets. Fest,

> Goebbels had ordered that a notice be posted on the door of every house, according to which, "by order of the *Führer* [...] all men between the ages of 15 and 70" should fulfil the call to the ranks, without exception. "Anyone who cowardly hides in the air-raid shelters," he concluded, "will end up in a court martial and will be punished with death" (FEST, 2005, p.38).

The Soviet waves of attack continue in Mission *Eviction.* Reznov makes it clear that the old, the young and the weak are now fighting for Germany in a desperate attempt to defend it. The player is also informed of the battle statistics: there are 45,000 German soldiers and 40,000 civilians fighting against 2.5 million Russian soldiers.

But, presented as thirsting for revenge, Reznov acclaims that "if they fight for Germany, they die for Germany". This mission begins with a scene in which a German soldier is sitting in a chair, surrounded by arguing Soviets:

- He wants mercy!
- You do not deserve mercy.
- What mercy did you show to our people!
- Time to die!
- Wait... Wait! He may help us.
- Help us? He can die for us.[92]

The German was then shot in the head with a rifle.

- Pfff. (one of the Soviet soldiers lets out a sigh)

[92] Translation: "He wants mercy! / You don't deserve mercy. / What mercy have you shown our people! / Time to die. / Wait... Wait! He can help us. / Help us? He can die for us".

- Mudak![93]

Chernov, indignant, vented: "This isn't war. This is murder. And Reznov replies: "That's how you end a war, Chernov". The Soviet soldiers who tried to spare the prisoner apparently resembled Chernov in their opinion of German prisoners - alluding to the fact that, just as not every German soldier was fanatical about Nazism, neither were many Soviet soldiers.

From then on, there is a passage in which a Russian soldier is also held prisoner by Germans, in a similar way to the scene at the beginning of the mission. The surrendered soldier promises that killing him won't save them, and that his mates won't show mercy. The German replies that his mates aren't there (which isn't true, as now the protagonist and his team are close by). Depending on the player's speed, the soldier being held prisoner may or may not be saved from execution. Scenes like this, which show how enemies treat their prisoners, are part of a critique of the Soviet and German methods, in contrast to the so-called liberating combat that the Americans proposed to be fair in the Pacific.

At the end of *Eviction,* there's another scene of brutality that relies on the player's concept of ethics: two surrendered German soldiers are about to be executed. Reznov gives Dimitri the choice: kill them quickly, with gunshots, or kill them slowly, with *Molotov* cocktails. Contrary to what the player might expect, however, Reznov reprimands Dimitri if the option of burning them is chosen. He says, in a reflective tone, that "it's cruel to prolong an animal's pain". In this moral truce, Reznov apparently understands his enemies as irrational creatures who don't know what they're doing: in this case, fighting for a repugnant ideal. It's almost as if he were feeling sorry for, as he himself suggests, "animals" about to be sacrificed. By opting for execution by shooting, on the other hand, Reznov praises the player/protagonist.

The last two missions of the campaign are directly connected: one in front of the *Reichstag* and the other inside it.

The penultimate one begins with Chernov writing in a diary. The sergeant

93 "Idiot" in Russian.

discourages him by asking: "What do you think will get us home? Writing about the war or winning it? No-one will ever read that" - and hands him a flag of the Soviet Union.

The scenery is as chaotic as possible: Berlin is smoke and ruins, and among the gunfire, German soldiers lie hanging from ghostly trees. The missiles of the *Katyusha*[94] devastate the buildings. A few metres into the film, the Reichstag becomes visible, separated by a long passage to its gates. Its path, however, is well-defended, and even SS soldiers fight against the Soviets. At one point, Chernov is killed by an enemy flamethrower; Reznov keeps his diary.

Depending on the player's actions during the missions, Chernov comes to different conclusions in his notes, cementing his profile as a mediating and rational soldier. If Dimitri divides his actions between Reznov's violent orders and his own conscience, sometimes sparing the enemy, Chernov concludes that heroes don't need to justify their actions, even if he doesn't understand them. If Dimitri follows all the sergeant's cruel orders, the diary reveals that the comrade is not a hero, but proposes that he is a savage, concluding that this would also be the case for the rest of the Red Army. But if Chernov realises that Dimitri is at all times merciful to the enemy, he considers him a true hero within the Soviet forces. However, the view of the sergeant remains the same, regardless of the player's choices: "Reznov, you seem to delight in slaughter". As already mentioned, while Chernov serves as Dimitri's good conscience, the bad one is personified through Sergeant Reznov. The words in the diary can move the player negatively or positively, depending on their choices during the course of the *game.*

The last mission takes place after the battle against the resistance outside the parliament and continues inside. A strong resistance is encountered, albeit made up of many wounded: several enemies have bloody bandages, but they fight without fear of death. Their deplorable condition does not allow the last mission to be completed

[94] Also known as "Stalin's Organ" by the Germans, it was a small lorry with a grid system that carried between 16 and 48 missiles, depending on the model. It is articulated, has a high rate of fire and was one of the best artillery weapons of the Second World War (LÚDEKE, 2009, p.184-185).

smoothly, as they are armed mainly with *STG's 44* and MG's 42. An allusion to Nazi symbolism is noticeable when, halfway through this mission, in the lobby of the parliament, a gigantic *Reichsadler* - the symbol of the eagle - has to be taken down by Dimitri with a *Panzerschrek.* The waves of enemies are endless as long as the Nazi symbol isn't destroyed; once it's down, however, the enemies stop attacking and the Soviets can continue. The *Reichsadler,* as in Figure 13, appears in the game as personification of Nazi fanaticism, and once it is destroyed, this ideological priority of protecting the Third *Reich* to the death is no longer present.

Figure 13: The *Reichsadler* in the *hall of* parliament. Available at: <http://i1-news.softpedia-static.com/images/extra/GAMES/large/COWAWtextscr_001-large.jpg>, accessed 13 Mar. 2017.

The *hall* where the eagle was located now serves as a meeting place for the German plenum, but during the Third *Reich*, it was a symbol of Nazi pride: in March 1933, Hitler gave a speech here after the approval of the "constitutional mandate law", or "law of full powers", which gave him legislative power for four years and symbolically marked the beginning of Nazi Germany (CLARET, 2006, p.52-53). In addition, the parliament had already been used as a pretext for the persecution of communists after the fire in February of the same year, although it is not known for sure whether this was really the cause or a plan by the Nazis themselves to increase support for Hitler (BUTLER, 2004, p.13). Perhaps for these reasons, the eagle in the *hall* signifies a symbol of struggle for the Germans featured in the *game* - because the whole context there represented, for Nazi ideology, the duration of twelve years of the Third *Reich.*

After passing through the *hall* and climbing up to the dome (which is also well protected), Dimitri and Reznov reach the *Reichstag* terrace and slowly advance to the edge. The player then witnesses a historic scene in the last seconds of the *game:* the flag of the Soviet Union is raised in place of the Nazi flag, celebrating the final victory of the Allies and the last battle for Europe. Reznov's plan for revenge seemed to have come to an end.

Figure 14 shows the photograph taken of soldier Abdoulkhakim Ismailov by Yevgeni Khaldei - Ismailov, like Dimitri, had fought since the counter-attack on Stalingrad. The portrait, on the other hand, was not spontaneous; it was the result of work carried out on 2 May to reproduce the record of the victory over Berlin on 30 April of that year (VALLS, 2009, p.28).

Figure 14: Photograph taken by Yevgeni Khaldei: Soviet soldier Ismailov poses for a photograph above the occupied Reichstag. Available at: <http://img.photobucket.com/albums/v642/antsmith/Reichstag_flag.jpg>, accessed 14 Mar. 2017.

The insertion of the Soviet flag over the Reichstag marked the end of a generation of this theme in the world of games, with the exception of a few franchises (Sniper Elite, for example, which had its most recent title released in February 2017). In turn, as already mentioned, perhaps the tendency of the producers of the current franchise is to return to the battles of yesteryear, given the strong influence that Battlefield 1 has exerted.

CHAPTER 4

Final considerations

From an analysis of the representations of the games analysed, one can see a huge preference for scenarios such as France, i.e. the geographical symbol of liberation, in which US troops played a special part; the primordial space of the Allied attack against the Axis; the first successful Allied invasion against the Germans. It's no surprise that the French scenario is emphasised. After all, it was there that the Americans began their offensive against the Nazi occupation. The American subject is so emphasised as the ideal of freedom that the games simply omit the fact that the United States has been involved in atrocities, such as the dropping of atomic bombs on Japanese cities, or the bombing of the German city of Dresden by the Americans and British in 1945. The emphasis on their proposed heroism thus omits the atrocities they committed, in order to emphasise their ideals of democracy in the face of Nazi-fascism.

On the other hand, given the cessation of the "World War II" theme among FPS games, there is also a strong inclination towards remakes[95] and continuations of old franchises, which appeal to beginners and veterans alike. These include Doom (Bethesda, 2016), Fallout 4 (Bethesda, 2015), Star Wars: Battlefront (EA, 2015), among others. Action games seem to have favoured rich dystopian themes.

Absolutely every electronic game, regardless of its year of release, genre and platform, is a potential object for the history researcher. The representations go far beyond iconography and iconology.

As a games researcher, I came to this conclusion when I was faced with new theoretical and methodological questions while writing my dissertation for a master's degree in History, where I prioritised the study of electronic games main character is science - using Valve's Half-Life series and Hideo Kojima and Konami's Metal Gear

[95] A concept used to refer to electronic games and cinema titles that have undergone complete remodelling in order to present experiences that are as impactful for players and viewers of today's generations as they were at the time of their original release.

Solid as the main objects.

In turn, since this is an object that conveys historical events, it is conceived that working with video games focused on this theme is a contribution to historical reflection on the subsequent representations constructed and conveyed about it. In order to overcome the difficulties encountered in achieving this objective, it was necessary to resort to the reflections proposed for working with other types of images, such as photography and cinema. In this sense, iconological and iconographic reading, which makes it possible to interpret contextual content presented solely through the image, is combined with reflection on the notion of representations.

In a general sense, however, there are an increasing number of contributions from historians in relation to games studies. In this career, I've come across the brilliant work of Karen Kremer (UEPG) and Luiz Gustavo Soares (UNIMONTES); I've also received valuable contributions from Dr Evanir Pavloski, from the Language Studies Department at UEPG; my master's supervisor, Antonio Paulo Benatte; Rogério Ivano, from the History Department at UEL; my supervisor during my undergraduate degree in History, Marco Stancik.

Researchers who contribute to the development of work on video games recognise that this object is underestimated. On the other hand, the variety of video games is vast and growing all the time. Electronic games developer Peter Molyneux states that:

> There was a world before games and a very different one afterwards. By making unbelievably sophisticated technology understandable and interactive in a matter of seconds, the change they brought about was immense. [...] Electronic games will continue to transform the world. We are living in a time of change and going through the most significant evolution in the history of games (MOLYNEUX, 2013, p.7).

Tony Mott is even more emphatic about these prejudices. Former editor-head of Edge, one of the biggest references on electronic games in the world.

United States, and a gamer for more than 30 years, makes it clear that the generic impression of video games is extremely immature:

> Compared to television, literature or music, the despised video game is not understood by many people. Perhaps we shouldn't expect it to be any different [...]. Books have been produced for hundreds of years, while films originated at the end of the 19th century. In comparative terms, in terms of their evolution, video games have already learnt to walk, but are only now starting to feed themselves without anyone's help. And just like children, who are often belittled or censored by repressive adults, games tend to be marginalised, generally appearing on the agenda of social commentators only when it's time for another round of condemnation (MOTT, 2013, p.8).

The transformation suggested by Molyneux, in dialogue with the non-understanding cited by Mott, probably concerns the way in which games will slowly and gradually interfere with cultures around the world. Perhaps optimistically, he suggests that games are gradually becoming vehicles for learning and knowledge, as opposed to notions of idleness or mere childish activities. These notions, built up during the 8-bit generation[96] , urgently need to be overcome. Play is one of humanity's oldest activities and should not be underestimated when it comes to virtual resources.

Once these difficulties have been overcome, researchers who dedicate themselves to games will find a vast universe of possibilities and questions. In terms of representations alone, there are countless research alternatives that can be found not only in history, but also in geography, psychology, music, the arts and pedagogy, among others. Given the number of titles and contexts that can be found in the universe of games, writing about them shouldn't be a problem; of course, if the researcher willing to work with such an object has the sensitivity to find the qualities and particularities of the subject.

of the *game* in question - again, regardless of its year of release, genre and platform.

Bibliographical references

ABRIL Collections (org). Suomi Model 31. In: Weapons of War Collection. São Paulo: Abril, v.15, 2010, p.152.

_____. Panzer III. In: Weapons of War Collection. São Paulo: Abril, v.10, 2010, p.117.

[96] The Atari 2600 and the *Nintendo Entertainment System* (NES, or "Nintendinho" in Brazil), for example. The term *bit*, short for *binary* digit, is used to designate the memory potential of a particular generation of video games.

ANKERSMIT, Frank. Representation and Reference, 2012. Available at: <https://bibliotecaonlinedahisfj.files.wordpress.com/2015/02/ankersmit-f-representac3a7c3a3o-e-referc3aancia.pdf>, accessed 03 Mar. 2017.

BASSETT, Richard. Admiral Canaris: Hitler's mysterious spy. Rio de Janeiro: Editora Nova Fronteira, 2005.

BELLIS, Mary. Computer and Video Game history. Available at: <http: //inventors .about. com/library/inventors/blcomputer_videogame s. htm>, accessed 03 Mar. 2017.

BIANCHIN, Victor; MITCH, Alinne (eds). How did consoles evolve? In: Mundo Estranho Collection: Everything you ever wanted to know about games. São Paulo: Abril, v.128-A, p.6-7, 2013.

BLAINEY, Geoffrey. A brief history of the world. São Paulo: Editora Fundamento Educacional, 2008.

BURKE, Peter. What is Cultural History? Rio de Janeiro: Zahar, 2008.

_____. Eyewitness: history and image. Bauru: EDUSC, 2004.

BURSTEIN, Laura. Panzer III versus Somua 35. *In: Collection 70th anniversary of World War II*. São Paulo: Abril Coleções, v.6, p. 25.

BUTLER, Rupert. *The Gestapo*: 1933-1939: The Founding of Hitler's Secret Police. São Paulo: Editora Escala, v.1, 2008.

CAILLOIS, Roger. *Games and Men*. Lisbon, Portugal: Edições Cotovia, 1990.

CALZAVARA, Bruno. *10 extraordinary acts of compassion in times of war*. Available at: < http://hypescience.com/10-atos-extraordinarios-de-compaixao-em-times-of-war/>, accessed 07 Mar. 2017.

CAMPBELL-KELLY, Martin. Christopher Strachey, 1985. Available at: <http://history.computer.org/pioneers/pdfs/S/Strachey.pdf>, accessed 03 Mar. 2017.

CAPELATO, Maria Helena. *Multidões em cena*: propaganda política no varguismo e peronismo. Campinas: Papirus, 1998.

CARDONA, Gabriel. The occupation of France. *In*: *70th anniversary of World War II collection*. São Paulo: Abril Coleções, 2009, v.6, p.7-33.

. The prelude to conflict. *In: Collection 70th anniversary of World War II*. São Paulo: Abril Coleções, v.1, p.20.

_____. Poland invaded. *In*: *Collection 70th anniversary of World War II*. São Paulo: Abril Coleções, v.2, p.7-29.

CHAGAS, Luciana. Captain America: Socio-anthropological Interpretations of a Comic Book Superhero. *In*: *SINAIS - Electronic journal*. Vitória: UFES, n.3, v.1, 2008, p.134-162.

CINE Players. *Rambo*: Programmed to kill. Available at: < http://www.cineplayers.com/filme/rambo--programado-para-matar/1327>, accessed 03 Mar. 2017.

CLARET, Martin (org). *Book-clipping*: Hitler for himself. São Paulo: Editora Martin Claret, 2006.

COMPUTER History Museum. Timeline of Computer History, 2006. Available at: <http://www.computerhistory.org/timeline/?category=cmptr>, accessed 03 Mar. 2017.

COSTILLA, Matías. The Seelow Hills, Berlin's last defensive barrier. *In*: *70th anniversary of World War II collection*. São Paulo: Abril Coleções, 2009, v.28, p.100-101.

DADGUM. *Ed Rotberg*. Available at: <http://www.dadgum.com/halcyon/BOOK/ROTBERG.HTM>, accessed 03 Mar. 2017.

DE PAULA, Cássio Remus. The submarine race: the technological rise of the Kriegsmarine submarines from 1919 to 1945. *In*: *Revista Marítima Brasileira*. Rio de Janeiro, v.134, n.10/12, p.107-117, 2014. Available at: < http://www.revistamaritima.com.br/sites/default/files/rmb-4-2014.pdf>, accessed 07 Mar. 2017.

_____. Videogames and Science Fiction: Representations of the chaotic future in electronic games of the 1980s. *In*: *Paths of History*. Montes Claros: Revista do Departamento de História UNIMONTES, 2015, v.20, n.2, p.89-114. Available in: <https://docs.google.com/viewer?a=v&pid=sites&srcid=ZGVmYXVsdGRvbWFpbn xyZXZpc3RhY2FtaW5ob3NkYWhpc3RvcmlhfGd4OjI1YjU0YWFjYWE0ZjNmYj Y>, accessed 13 Mar. 2017.

DUVIGNAUD, Jean. *The Game of the Game*. Santafé de Bogotá, Colombia: Fondo de Cultura Económica LTDA, 1997.

ELITE UK Forces. *Special Air Services (SAS)* - History (1941-1979). Available at:< http://www.eliteukforces.info/special-air-service/history/>, accessed 03 Mar. 2017.

EVANS, Richard. All hailed: the meaning of the Hitler salute. Available at: <http://www.nysun.com/arts/all-hailed-the-meaning-of-the-hitler-salute/74744/>. Accessed 13 Feb. 2017.

FALLSCHIRMJAGER. American items: M1C Airborne helmet 506 PIR 101 ABN. Available at: <http://www.fallschirmjager.biz/store_american0013.htm>, accessed 03 Mar. 2017.

FERRANTI Computer Systems. History, 2013. Available at: <http://www.ferranti.be/en/history>, accessed 10 Mar. 2015.

FEST, Joachim. In Hitler's bunker. Rio de Janeiro: Objetiva, 2005.

GALEANO, Luis. The greatest amphibious assault in the Pacific. *In: Collection 70th anniversary of World War II*. São Paulo: Abril Coleções, 2009, v.29, p.129-135.

____ . The importance of Okinawa for the Allies. *In*: *Collection 70th anniversary of World War II*. São Paulo: Abril Coleções, 2009, v.29, p.119-125.

____ . Assault on the Japanese fortresses of the Palau Islands. *In*: *Collection 70th anniversary of World War II*. São Paulo: Abril Coleções, 2009, v.29, p.37-63.

____ . The fall of Singapore and the conquest of the Gilbert Islands. *In*: *Collection 70th anniversary of World War II*. São Paulo: Abril Coleções, 2009, v.13, p.85-121.

GALLO, Sérgio Nesteriuk. *Gaming as an element of culture*: contemporary aspects and changes in the gaming experience, 2007. PhD Thesis in Communication and Semiotics. Postgraduate Studies Programme in Communication and Semiotics. Pontifical Catholic University, São Paulo. Available at: <http://livros01.livrosgratis.com.br/cp032117.pdf>, accessed 03 Mar. 2017.

GELLATELY, Robert. *In*: GOLDENSOHN, Leon. *The Nuremberg Interviews*. São Paulo: Companhia das Letras, 2005.

GIBSON, Ellie. Consoles. *In*: *Guinness World Records 2009: Games*. São Paulo: Ediouro, 2009, p.16-31.

GOMBRICH, Ernst. *Towards a Cultural History*. Lisbon: Gradiva, 1994.

GOMES, Beto. Operation Barbarossa. *In*: *Great Wars*: Everything new at the front. São Paulo: Abril, v.27, 2009, p.37-55.

GRAETZ, J. Martin. The origin of Spacewar. *In*: *Creative Computing Magazine*. New Jersey: Creative Computing, 1981. Available at: < http://www.wheels.org/spacewar/creative/SpacewarOrigin.html>, accessed 03 Mar. 2017.

GUNS.COM. *Winchester Model 1897*, 2017. Available at: < http://www.guns.com/reviews/winchester-model-1897/>, accessed 03 Mar. 2017.

HOBSBAWM, Eric. *Age of Extremes:* The brief twentieth century - 1914-1991. São Paulo: Companhia das Letras, 1995.

HORSFALL, Robin. John McAleese - man who made SAS famous, 2011. Available at: <http://www.thesun.co.uk/sol/homepage/features/3780753/John-McAleese-the-man-who-made-the-SAS-famous.html>, accessed 03 Mar. 2017.

HUIZINGA, Johann. *Homo Ludens*. São Paulo: Editora Perspectiva S.A., 2000.

JAPAN Atlas. *Shuri Castle*. Available at: <http://web-japan.org/atlas/historical/his25.html>, accessed 03 Mar. 2017.

JORGENSEN, Christer (ed.). *Great Battles*: Decisive conflicts that have shaped

History. Bath: Parragon, 2007.

JURADO, Carlos. The excessive demands of the Treaty of Versailles. *In: 70th anniversary of World War II collection*. São Paulo: Abril Coleções, 2009, v.1, p.31-37.

____ . Japanese expansion during the Sino-Japanese War. *In*: *Collection 70th anniversary of World War II*. São Paulo: Abril Coleções, 2009, v.1, p.87-93.

KLEINA, Nilton. What is an engine or graphics engine?, 2011. Available at: <http://www.tecmundo.com.br/video-game/9263-o-que-e-engine-ou-motor-grafico-.htm>, accessed 03 Mar. 2017.

KOSSOY, Boris. *Photography and history*. São Paulo: Ateliê Editorial, 2001.

KRPATA, Mitch. Pong. *In*: *1001 video games to play before you die*. Rio de Janeiro: Sextante, p.23, 2013.

LIPPE, Pedro Henrique. *Studio wants "Call of Duty: Infinite Warfare" to win back lost fans*, 2016. Available at: <https://jogos.uol.com.br/ultimas-noticias/2016/05/02/estudio-quer-que-call-of-duty-infinite-warfare-recupere-fas-perdidos.htm>, accessed 14 Mar. 2017.

LOSADA, Juan Carlos. The photograph of the American flag on Iwo Jima. *In: 70th anniversary of World War II collection*. São Paulo: Abril Coleções, v.29, p.18-19, 2009.

____ . Stalin's Great Purge of the Red Army. *In*: *Collection 70th anniversary of World War II*. São Paulo: Abril Coleções, 2009, v.3, p.11.

LÚDEKE, Alexander. *Weapons of World War II*. Bath: Parragon, 2011.

MARTIN, Douglas. *Hélène Deschamps Adams, wartime hero, dies at 85*, 2006. Available at: <http://www.nytimes.com/2006/09/24/nyregion/23deschamps.html>, accessed 14 Feb. 2017.

MEDAL Of Honor Wiki. *Tiger Tank*. Available at: < http://medalofhonor.wikia.com/wiki/Tiger_tank>, accessed 03 Mar. 2017.

MERETSKOV, Kiril. The evolution of artillery, 2014. Available at: < http://www.clubedosgenerais.org/site/artigos/96/2014/06/a-evolucao-da-artilharia/>, accessed 03 Mar. 2017.

MILITARY Factory. Flakpanzer IV Wirbelwind (Whirlwind) Self-Propelled Anti-Aircraft Gun Platform, 2016. Available at: < http://www.militaryfactory.com/armor/detail.asp?armor_id=712>, accessed 03 Mar. 2017.

MOORHOUSE, Roger. I want to kill Hitler. São Paulo: Ediouro, 2009.

MULLER, Lutz. The *Hero:* We are all born to be heroes. São Paulo: Cultrix Publishing House, 1987.

NARLOCH, Leandro. Hiroshima, the Abominable New World. *In*: *Adventures in History*. São Paulo: Abril, 2005, v.24, p.28-35.

NATIONAL WW2 Museum. *African Americans in World War II*: Fighting for a double victory. Available at: <http://www.nationalww2museum.org/assets/pdfs/african-americans-in-world.pdf>, accessed 06 Mar. 2017.

ONÇA, Fabiano. D-Day: The invasion of Normandy. *In*: *Great Wars Collection*. São Paulo: Abril, 2005, v.6, p.6-7.

OSS Society. Available at: <http://www.osssociety.org/>, accessed 03 Mar. 2017.

PANOFSKY, Erwin. *Iconology and iconography*: An introduction to the study of Renaissance art. *In*: *Meaning in the Visual Arts*. São Paulo: Perspectiva, 1986, p.47-65.

PLESHAKOV, Constantine. *Stalin's Madness*. Rio de Janeiro: DIFEL, 2008.

POLLAK, Michael. Memory and social identity. *In*: *Historical Studies*. Rio de Janeiro, 1992, v.5, n.10, p. 200-212. Available at: <http://bibliotecadigital.fgv.br/ojs/index.php/reh/article/view/1941/1080>, accessed 14 Feb. 2017.

REGALADO, Marcelo. Soviet advance in Berlin: the struggle for the Reichstag. *In*: *70th anniversary of World War II collection.* São Paulo: Abril Coleções, 2009, v.28, p.120.

RIBEIRO, Flávia. Saving Private Ryan. *In: Adventures in History - Great Wars*: 100 Best War Films of All Time. São Paulo: Abril, n.60- A, 2008, p.19.

SKORUPA, Francisco Alberto. *Journey to the Letters of the Future*. Curitiba: Aos Quatro Ventos, 2002.

ROMANA, José Miguel. *Hitler's secret weapons*. São Paulo: Madras, 2010.

RYBACK, Timothy. Hitler's forgotten library: The books that shaped the Fuhrer's life. São Paulo: Companhia das Letras, 2009.

SALKELD, Luke. Rommel saved me from being shot as a spy, 2014. Available at: < http://www.dailymail.co.uk/news/article-2842467/Rommel-saved-shot-spy-served-cigarettes-beer-WW2-veteran-95-reveals-astonishing-story-survival-pre-D-Day-mission.html>, accessed 07 Mar. 2017.

SHOEMAKER, Richie. War. In: Guinness World Records 2009: Games. São Paulo: Ediouro, 2009, p.38-55.

SOLER, José Ramón. How Poland broke the Enigma machine code. In: *Collection 70th anniversary of World War II.* São Paulo: Abril Coleções, 2009 v.2, p.132-133.

STEIW, Leandro. The Great Dictator. In: *Great Wars Collection*. São Paulo: Abril: 2008, v.60, p.64.

SVITRAS, Caroline. *The dangerous atomic programme that Germany developed in World War II*·2017. Available at:< http://leiturasdahistoria.uol.com.br/o- dangerous-atomic-programme-that-germany-developed-in-the-2nd-world-war/>, accessed 03 Mar. 2017.

TILLION, Germaine. *In*: CUNHA, Maria. Literature and journalism in Agnès' war. *In*: *Proceedings of the Women and Literature Seminar*. Brasília: UnB, 2011, v.1, n.1.

TOTA, Antonio Pedro. *Seductive Imperialism*: The Americanisation of Brazil at the time of the Second War. São Paulo: Companhia das Letras, 2000.

UOL Jogos. *The history of video games*: 1961. Available at: <http://jogos.uol.com.br/reportagens/historia/1961.jhtm>, accessed 03 Mar. 2017.

. *The history of video games:* 1971 - 1974. Available at: <http://jogos.uol.com.br/reportagens/historia/1971.jhtm>, accessed 03 Mar. 2017.

VALLS, Mar (Org). *Folha Great Photographers Collection*: War. São Paulo: Folha de São Paulo, 2009, p. 28.

VÁZQUEZ, Juan. The Battle of Britain was not a "Blitzkrieg". *In: Collection 70th anniversary of World War II*. São Paulo: Abril Coleções, 2009, v.9, p.127-136.

____ . The Allies retreat in the face of the German Panzers. *In*: *Collection 70th anniversary of World War II*. São Paulo: Abril Coleções, 2009, v.6, p.99-123.

____ . The end of the beginning or the beginning of the end. *In*: *Collection 70th anniversary of World War II*. São Paulo: Abril Coleções, 2009, v.30, p.101-109.

VISUAL Thinking: Anyforms. The Blitzkrieg theory. *In*: *Collection 70th anniversary of World War II*. São Paulo: Abril Coleções, 2009, v.2, p.20-21.

VITORIA, Rodrigo Diaz. The *Germans try to reverse the situation. In: Collection 70th anniversary of World War II*. São Paulo: Abril Coleções, 2009, v.27, p.35-47

WARBIRD Alley. *Douglas C-47 Skytrain/Dakota*. Available at: <http://www.warbirdalley.com/c47.htm>, accessed 03 Mar. 2017.

WILLMOT, H.P. *Second World War*. Rio de Janeiro: Nova Fronteira, 2008.

WINTER, David. *Pong History*, 2013. Available at: <http://www.pong-story.com/odyssey.htm#P5>, accessed 03 Mar. 2017.

WORLD Guns. *Armalite / Colt AR-15 / M16 M16A1 M16A2 M16A3 M16A4 assault rifle (USA)*. Available at: <http://modernfirearms.net/assault/usa/m16-m16a1- m16a2-

m16a3-e.html>, accessed 03 Mar. 2017.

____ . *Panzerfaust*: Faustpatrone antitank grenade launchers (Germany). Available at: < http://modernfirearms.net/grenade/de/panzerfaust-e.html>, accessed 03 Mar. 2017.

YOSHIDA, Ernesto (ed). Circle of Fire. *In: Adventures in History - Great Wars*: 100 Best War Films of All Time. São Paulo: Abril, n.60-A, 2008, p.38.

Printed by Books on Demand GmbH, Norderstedt / Germany